TITANIC

...And the Strange Case of Great Uncle Bertie

TITANIC

...And the Strange Case
of Great Uncle Bertie

VALENTINE PALMER

TITANIC

…And the Strange Case of Great Uncle Bertie

fantom
publishing

First published in 2012 by Fantom Films
fantomfilms.co.uk

A catalogue record for this book is available from the British Library.

Hardback Edition ISBN: 978-1-906263-78-2

Typeset by Phil Reynolds Media Services, Leamington Spa
Printed by MPG Biddles Limited, King's Lynn

Jacket design by Iain Robertson

Photographs appear on plates between pages 86 and 87.

For Catherine

Contents

FOREWORD   1

PART ONE – MY FAMILY AND THE *TITANIC*

Chapter 1: The Lightollers   6

The funeral – A place of mysteries – A lesson in colour – Grandma
Gertrude – The press clippings

Chapter 2: The family and Great Uncle Bertie   11

The coat of arms – Hampstead Garden Suburb – The Blitz –
My mother and her Uncle Bertie – Meetings with the great man –
The attraction of the sea – Heroes and villains – Everyone knows
the *Titanic*

Chapter 3: *Titanic* in the movies and on television   19

Cashing in on disaster – The Nazi *Titanic* – *A Night to Remember* –
Keeping the drama alive – Cameron hits the jackpot – *Doctor Who*,
the *Titanic* and me

Chapter 4: Bertie's adventurous life   27

What price progress? – Tragic childhood – First experience of ice –
Storm at sea – Shipwreck – A deserted island – The lure of gold –
Riding the range – More cattle

Chapter 5: Love, luck and Christian Science   36

Marriage – What is luck? – Lightoller and Christian Science – Sylvia
and Christian Science

Chapter 6: Ireland, danger and scandal   41

My Irish grandfather – A fishy story – What to do with the boy – A
perilous crossing – Emergency – U-boat! – Passengers in danger –
Another family scandal – Lightoller's place in the scheme of things

PART TWO – SURVIVORS AND COURTROOM DRAMAS

Chapter 7: The White Star Line and Lightoller   50

The appeal of *Titanic* – The Ismays – Ismay and the tennis champ – Lightoller and his nemesis – The rescue ship reaches New York – A view from the press

Chapter 8: Survivors and their stories   57

'The black family' – Kidnapped – Jack Thayer's story – Romance – 'The Unsinkable Molly Brown' – The Waldorf-Astoria – Who are the bad guys?

Chapter 9: Let the trial begin   64

The basic facts – Warning! Ice! – Corporate-speak! – 'Go to Hell!' – 'Watertight' Smith – Lightoller's opinion

Chapter 10: Unexpected revelations   72

Senator Smith loses patience – George Harder's testimony – Failure to close the watertight doors – Lifeboat chaos – Icebergs everywhere!

Chapter 11: Cross-examination   80

Ismay on the spot – The Second Officer v Senator Smith – Unanswered questions – The sea trials – Unhelpful Lightoller – Lightoller and lifeboats – Only six lifeboats tested

Chapter 12: Dodging the question   88

No recommendations – Searchlights – Lookouts – Lightoller talks with Ismay – The strange case of Luis Klein – The stowaway – The press and the mysterious Mr Klein – Klein sounds the alarm – The disappearance of Mr Klein

Chapter 13: Confused evidence   96

More questions – The British inquiry – Which Marconigram? – Full speed in an ice field! – Women and children first! – Missing messages

Chapter 14: Important witnesses   103

Members of the Board – Enter Sir Ernest Shackleton – Dark icebergs – Sighting an iceberg – The lifeboat disaster – The Master of the *Carpathia*

Chapter 15: Ismay's part in the drama   109

Ismay and Lightoller – Giants of the sea – The cost of a *Titanic* ticket – Ismay accused – The crucial telegram – Ismay in love

PART THREE – STORIES AND CONSPIRACIES

Chapter 16: Death and Divine Power   116

Into the spotlight – The plot thickens – Two old ladies at a funeral – Goodbye Bertie, goodbye Bruce – A Christian Scientist's view – Lightoller gets it wrong – Divine Power

Chapter 17: Omissions   125

Avoidance – Riches indeed – Not the ideal captain – The dream ship – What went wrong? – Ice warnings – *Titanic*'s first disaster – Lightoller reads the stars – Bertie is confused – What really happened?

Chapter 18: Lady Louise reveals all   135

A family secret – Confusion at the wheel – More lies? – Unanswered questions – True and false stories – More conflicting stories – Jumping ship

Chapter 19: The drama of the *Olympic*   146

Leading actors in the drama – The shooting – The strange case of the *Olympic* – No money for White Star – Patching up *Olympic* – Conspiracies the world over

Chapter 20: It's all about money   153

Priceless artefacts – Losing money hand over fist – Problem with the rivets – The 'switch' – Enter the Royal Navy – The *Olympic* lives on – The *Olympic* at war – Reasons for the 'switch' – Robert Ballard and the *Titanic*

PART FOUR – FRAUD AND OUR HERO

Chapter 21: A possible 'switch'   162

The reasons for the 'switch' – Maritime fraud – The big secret – A picture tells a story – Reasons to be doubtful – Who wants to go on a maiden voyage? – Ghost ships – Insuring *Titanic* – Choosing the wrong route – Warnings that went unheeded

Chapter 22: Who sank the ship?   169

Fraud at sea – *Titanic*'s last hours – A question of lookouts – Why did the *Californian* stop? – How to sink a ship – Iceberg or mystery ship? – A glancing blow – Marian Thayer and the mystery ship – Why not start the pumps?

Chapter 23: A recipe for disaster 178

The mystery deepens – The call goes unanswered – No lifeboat drill – *Carpathia* to the rescue – Truth and the *Carpathia* – Captain Smith's final mistake – A hero with 'feet of clay'? – What did Grandma Gertrude not tell me? – Outside the box – We are all human

AFTERWORD 187

What the public wants – Big ideas – Thrust into centre stage – Saved by the war – An unsuitable posting – A ship of his own – Vile sharks! – No place for Lightoller – *Sundowner* – Spies! – Dunkirk – A legend again – *Lux Vestra*: Let Your Light Shine

ACKNOWLEDGEMENTS 196

REFERENCES AND FURTHER READING 197

Foreword

This is a story of a man and a ship. Millions of people across the world have, for the past hundred years, been convinced that they know the story of the *Titanic*. On its maiden voyage from Southampton to New York it hit an iceberg and sank with horrific loss of life. However, if you were to ask how a magnificent liner – built regardless of expense and owned by a prestigious British shipping company – could come to such a catastrophic end, comparatively few will be able to answer.

My great uncle, Charles Herbert Lightoller, was the most senior surviving officer of the tragedy. As the Second Officer on the doomed liner, after the sinking he found himself thrust into the spotlight of two official inquiries, one in the US and one in Britain. At neither of these did he acquit himself well; yet neither he, nor any of the senior officers who were lost, were in any way censured for what had befallen the ship that many considered 'unsinkable'.

Although, as a young boy, I met Commander Lightoller on several occasions, I recall no talk amongst the family of the *Titanic* or my great uncle's involvement in the sinking. Perhaps everyone felt that he should be allowed to forget the terrible event. But how could he forget such a traumatic experience? And the world certainly didn't want to forget it either. Countless books, films and television programmes have endlessly regurgitated the events of that dreadful night. When I was approached to write a book about the great ship and the 'great man', I felt somewhat overawed by the seemingly

inexhaustible wealth of material already covering the subject –
except that most of this coverage concerned the planning,
building, launching and sinking of the ship, and not that much
had anything to do with Second Officer Lightoller. Of course
there was my great uncle's autobiography *Titanic and Other
Ships*, which seemed to be mainly a catalogue of these 'other
ships' and also contained one or more glaring inaccuracies.
Also, Patrick Stenson had written *'Lights': The Odyssey of C. H.
Lightoller*, a fascinating account of my great uncle's
adventurous life. But on the whole, writers and researchers
seem focused on the actual sinking, rather than how Lightoller
managed to survive the disaster when other senior officers did
not. Also, very few comment on his extraordinary behaviour at
the official investigations immediately after the disaster.

As I began my search for anything that would reveal more
about my great uncle and his life before, during and after the
loss of the great ship, childhood memories began to emerge
from the dim recesses of my mind. There were fragments of
conversations with my maternal grandmother (Lightoller's
sister), my mother, and her father – a man overshadowed by
scandal and secrecy, but with a revealing link to one of
Titanic's lasting mysteries.

One of the difficulties facing any serious student of the
Titanic tragedy is not only the mass of information available
but within it the vast amount of conflicting testimony from
survivors, amplified and embellished down the generations.
Add to these the exaggerated and often inaccurate reports in
the contemporary press, and I trust that readers of this book
will appreciate the daunting task that faced me of sifting the
truth from the merely fanciful. There can be no doubt that
Charles Herbert Lightoller was an extraordinary man. He was
tough, he was brave and he appeared to take storm, shipwreck
and official enquiries in his stride. However, in seeking to
answer some of the unanswered questions about the *Titanic*
and her loss, I have found myself uncovering family secrets
and scandals that both directly and indirectly influenced my

opinions about the most famous of all maritime losses. I must hasten to point out that any conclusions I appear to reach about my great uncle's conduct during and after the sinking, together with ideas formed regarding the behaviour of the owners and officials of the *Titanic*, are based solely on my personal researches, together with memories recalled from childhood.

Great Uncle Bertie, as I came to call him through my Grandma Gertrude's influence, is as fascinating a character as any well-drawn hero brought to life by great writers of fiction. He was heroic and yet, when the occasion required it, he may well have been a liar. Truth is sometimes much stranger than fiction; and the short life of the ship called *Titanic*, and to a great extent Great Uncle Bertie's adventures on sea and on land, are a living proof of this.

Second Officer Lightoller always maintained that his survival in the *Titanic*'s sinking, when some fifteen hundred other souls perished, was directly attributable to his faith in a higher power; a belief he had arrived at through his conversion to the tenets of Christian Science. It is certainly an interesting footnote to the tragic sinking on April 15th 1912 that Great Uncle Bertie went on to further exciting adventures in both the First and Second World War. These included sinking a German U-boat, shooting a Zeppelin airship, acting as a spy, and rescuing over a hundred soldiers pinned down by enemy fire on the beaches of Dunkirk. What a man!

And what of the other key players in the *Titanic* drama? Well, J. Bruce Ismay, considered by many to be the driving force behind all that was wrong with the *Titanic* – as well as being to my mind Great Uncle Bertie's nemesis – completely disappeared from the scene, a broken man; while the fabulously wealthy J. Pierpont Morgan, the ultimate owner of the White Star Line under whose flag the *Titanic* sailed, died the year following the sinking. So I think we could safely say that, despite the very real possibility of Lightoller having been encouraged to perjure himself at some point, the man was a survivor in every sense of the word.

There can probably never be final closure to the story of the *Titanic* and the strange case of Great Uncle Bertie. Too much time has elapsed and too many stories, myths and theories have been created over the past hundred years. This book is merely my attempt to provide a fair and balanced account of events as I perceive them. It is also the story of a remarkable member of my family of whom Grandma Gertrude so aptly remarked:

'Most people thought my brother was a hero. Well, in a way he was; but after all – we're all human.'

Valentine Palmer
Brighton
February 2012

Part One
My Family and the *Titanic*

Chapter 1
The Lightollers

The funeral

A chill December wind made waves across the broad reach of the Thames by Mortlake Bridge. Naked trees swayed limb-like branches across the edge of a grim red-brick building, into which trooped a steady procession of black-clad figures. There was me – a skinny thirteen-year-old in a suit that looked made for a bigger person.

The vicar in charge droned on about the 'great man', his adventurous life, his courage and bravery through peace and in war, his family, his widow and his sister. But of course he didn't mention me – or my mother. There the two of us sat, wedged between Grandma Gertrude, the great man's sister and Great Aunt Sylvia, his widow. My mother was having a good weep, the way she always liked to. The two upright old ladies either side of us showed little or no sign of grieving. They were made of sterner stuff.

We watched the doors of the furnace open, the coffin move into the flames and my great uncle, Charles Herbert Lightoller, hero of the *Titanic*'s tragic sinking, left our lives for ever. He took with him the unsolved mysteries of the loss of the great ship and his part in it. What he did leave behind was a well-documented catalogue of his adventurous life and heroism – or were there some tales left untold? Were there riddles yet to be solved?

6

A place of mysteries

Over the years, my interest in the *Titanic* and its tragic end grew until it became quite an obsession with me. On a number of occasions before they died I tried to get some information on the subject from both my grandmother, Gertrude, and my great aunt, Sylvia. Grandma Gertrude intimated to me that the full truth of the *Titanic*'s demise had never been made public. However, she only seemed willing to speak of the event in riddles, the meaning of most of which has only begun to become clearer as my research for this book has progressed. Remarks like:

'The sea is a place of mysteries – and there are mystery ships upon it.'

It was to be many years before I stumbled upon the possible explanation of this riddle: an explanation so horrific that, if true, it would almost dwarf the tragedy of the great liner's sinking.

Great Aunt Sylvia, on the other hand, more or less clammed right up on the rare occasions that I visited her and broached the subject. So, once I was approached to write a book about my great uncle and his involvement in the *Titanic*'s sinking, I began to try to fit the pieces of the puzzle together. And a long and complex task it turned out to be.

My eccentric grandmother liked to be known as Gertrude Lightoller, as opposed to Gertrude Hannah, her original married name. Her attachment to the Lightoller name was a strong one, as she often spoke of her brother, Commander Lightoller, or Bertie as she always called him.

A lesson in colour

I remember the first time Grandma Gertrude brought out her book of French Impressionists and told me to half close my eyes and look at the works of Monet, Renoir and the others. In doing so, I found the pictures becoming much clearer, taking on an almost three-dimensional quality. Grandma Gertrude also taught me about colour.

'What colour is the sky?' she asked me one day.

When I answered that it was blue, she took me out into her small back garden.

'Look at that bit of sky over there!' she commanded. 'What colour is it?'

'A sort of blue,' I replied, for it was a fine, clear summer day.

'Now make a little shape like this,' she said, making a small viewfinder of her cupped hand – just the way I would, in later years, when considering a shot I wanted in a movie.

'Now what colour is it?' she asked.

I looked at the sky again, this time through my improvised viewfinder; and, lo and behold, the little patch of sky that I now saw was full of different colours – blue, yes, but also purple, pink, grey and more.

'It's lots of different colours!' I shouted in excitement.

'Exactly!' laughed my grandmother. 'You saw the sky as blue because you've always been told that the sky is blue. Just because people tell you something is so, it doesn't necessarily mean that what they say is true. Most people believe what they're told to believe because then they don't have to think for themselves.'

Thus, at an early age, I learned that things in life are not always what you've been led to believe they are; and many years later I was to discover that this was certainly true of the *Titanic* and its tragic end.

Grandma Gertrude

Grandma Gertrude wore coloured ribbons in her grey hair because she had a thing about colour. Her clothes, the pictures she painted – everything about her and her surroundings was colourful, including her two little dogs which also had coloured ribbons in their hair. I remember thinking that these were not my idea of a proper dog. A proper dog was one like the bull terrier we had at home at the time. Years later, when I was playing Bill Sikes in the musical *Oliver!* in London's West

End, I acquired Sikes' ferocious bull terrier, Bullseye. I reckon he'd have had my grandmother's little dogs for breakfast!

In the years that I knew her, Grandma Gertrude lived alone. I learned that in her younger days she had married a churchman from Northern Ireland, moved there and produced three daughters – my mother, Elizabeth, and her two sisters, Theodora and Eunice. However, it was never explained to me why my mother's father, Canon Hannah, as he then was, lived in Ireland and Grandma Gertrude lived in London. Although my mother and I spent some time with the Canon in Northern Ireland when I was very young, nothing was ever properly explained to me until, when I was much older, Great Aunt Sylvia took it upon herself to reveal the scandal that had rent the family apart and left my mother consumed with the bitterness that I sensed in her until her dying day.

The press clippings

When we went to visit Grandma Gertrude in Hampstead Garden Suburb, my parents would usually disappear into one of the adjoining cottages to take tea and chat with one or other of my aunts. This seemed more important to my mother than spending time with her mother. When my parents did occasionally stop to chat with Grandma Gertrude, knowing how easily a young person can get bored with adult conversation, my grandmother usually suggested that I go into her study to look at her collection of magazines, which she knew held a strange fascination for me. The reason for my interest was that many of these magazines were over thirty years old. There were back copies of the *Tatler*, the *Illustrated London News* and other periodicals I had never heard of. They were full of ladies in strange dresses, motor cars that I considered to be ancient, and other extraordinary fashions from what seemed like a bygone age.

While reading these magazines in her study, my eye was invariably drawn to a tall oak cupboard with a key in the door. If you don't want young boys to look in your cupboard, then you should not leave the key in the lock, because it will be absolutely irresistible to them. I was certainly no exception. So, one day I crept over to the cupboard and turned the key in the lock and, lo and behold, the door opened! Inside the cupboard there were a number of shoeboxes filled with old newspaper clippings. Imagine my surprise when I found that many of these were even older than the ancient magazines I had been studying. They were somewhat faded and dog-eared but nevertheless readable, so I abandoned the old magazines in favour of investigating the contents of Grandma Gertrude's shoe boxes. The clippings all related to the same incident – the sinking of the *Titanic*. As I thumbed through the cuttings, there it all was: 'TITANIC SINKS', 'TERRIBLE TITANIC DISASTER', 'GREAT LOSS OF LIFE', and many more similar headlines. Fearful of discovery, I closed the cupboard again and rejoined my parents and my grandmother, resolving never to tell anyone about the discovery I had made in Grandma Gertrude's locked cupboard.

So when I was asked to write a book about the Second Officer on the doomed *Titanic*, how could I refuse? Except that I then found myself with a series of questions that appear to have remained largely unanswered for the past hundred years. In fact it actually seemed more like a collection of mysteries. So, where was I to start? The hero, of course, would be my great uncle, Charles Herbert Lightoller, always referred to as Uncle Herbert by my mother, while to my father he was 'the Commander'. It appears that his seagoing chums referred to him as 'Lights'.

Chapter 2
The family and
Great Uncle Bertie

The coat of arms

Grandma Gertrude displayed the Lightoller coat of arms in a prominent position above the mantlepiece of her modest cottage in London's Hampstead Garden Suburb. A copy of the coat of arms that she drew and hand-painted for me was the result of the drawing lessons that she gave me. During these she would often say to me:

'When you draw, don't try to draw everything you see. Life is a series of impressions.'

That said, the Lightoller coat of arms she created for me was certainly not impressionistic, but executed with the utmost skill and precision. For many years this very coat of arms, with its brief motto *Lux Vestra* ('let your light shine'), has hung on the wall above my desk. Until I started my researches for this book about Great Uncle Bertie I had not given it much thought. Now I began to look at it in a fresh light. I remember Grandma Gertrude drawing the coat of arms with such great care, colouring it in with the paints that she always kept close by her. Unlike many an elderly lady I had met, she was able to wield her pen and brushes with youthful dexterity. A golden lion rampant quickly appeared on the shield surmounted by a knight's helmet with visor closed.

Later research revealed that the Lightoller family were Lords of the Manor in Lancashire as early as the thirteenth century. I certainly wanted a coat of arms of my own. So I took this up with my grandmother:

'Do I have a coat of arms, Grandma?' I remember asking her.

'I'm afraid not, dear. You see, although your mummy is a Lightoller, she married your father, Henry Palmer, and he doesn't have a coat of arms.'

'But doesn't everyone have a coat of arms?'

'No, dear – only really old families.'

I later discovered that 'old' families were the ones with power and influence, or at least that's what they thought they had.

'So, if mummy had married someone else, then I could have had a coat of arms?'

'Exactly. But you are going to have one, because I'm doing this one for you.'

I gazed at the thick art paper where my grandmother was putting the finishing touches to the picture. I was excited but confused. It seemed that Grandma Gertrude was giving me a wonderful present, but something that was not truly mine. Later it was carefully framed and glassed by my father, and kept in what was considered a safe place – hanging in our hall beside the Victorian hatstand. I wonder how my father, a self-made successful businessman, felt about marrying – as Grandma Gertrude probably thought – 'above himself'.

Hampstead Garden Suburb

As I look at it now, with its worn wood frame and slightly parchment-looking image, I realise that my grandmother, Gertrude Lightoller, who never answered to her married name of Hannah, was what my father probably considered to be 'a bit of a snob'. She lived in a fashionable cottage in a very middle-class *cul-de-sac* in Hampstead Garden Suburb. This area, designed and built in the very early twentieth century, was intended as an example of tasteful yet affordable dwellings for 'all classes and all incomes'. Set just a few miles from the centre of London, this 'garden city' was the pride of its architects and builders. These quaint, fake rural retreats just six miles from St Paul's Cathedral are now much sought after by upwardly mobile individuals from the City of London, able, through their bountiful bonuses, to pay for a 'three up – two down' in the leafy arcadia of this early twentieth-century dream.

Either side of my grandmother's cottage sat similar dwellings occupied by my two aunts, Eunice and Theodora, who formed, together with my mother Elizabeth, the remains of a tragic marriage between my grandmother and my grandfather, the Reverend William Hannah. The scandals of the Lightollers and the Hannahs were unknown to me until revealed by Great Aunt Sylvia long after her husband's death and when I was well into adulthood. Some families seem to have rather more than their fair share of drama, tragedy and scandal. The Lightollers were one such family. Perhaps it's what some people might call *karma*.

The Blitz

For some considerable time after World War Two, many of Britain's cities lay in ruins from the German bombers' onslaught that failed to conquer the country, but left its population almost as badly off as their defeated enemy. My parents had moved into the country at the onset of the Blitz, but most of their relations on both sides of the family had elected to remain in the city. I have quite vivid memories of my father driving my mother and me past bombed-out buildings and piles of rubble on our way to visit relatives long after the war had finished. Grandma Gertrude and my two aunts remained unscathed – for what strategic importance could possibly be placed on Hampstead Garden Suburb?

However, the Palmer side of the family had been less fortunate and suffered terribly in their proximity to the

London docks. Relatives who had been lost were mentioned only briefly by my parents, although family funerals seemed to figure heavily in my earliest remembrances. I certainly recall how transfixed I was on meeting a young cousin who had lost her parents in a bombing raid and also, tragically, lost her sight as well. She never seemed to stop crying, despite my hopeless entreaties for her to do so.

My mother and her Uncle Bertie

My father's mother and father had died before I was born and my mother's father lived in Ireland. When you are a child you don't usually think of querying unusual family arrangements. Although my mother constantly spoke glowingly of her father, he was never mentioned in my grandmother's presence.

I was absolutely fascinated by the clippings about the *Titanic* that I had discovered in Grandma Gertrude's cupboard and although I never revealed my findings to her, one day I did broach the subject of the *Titanic* with my mother and she announced emphatically:

'Your great uncle was a hero, he saved hundreds of people.' My mother warmed to her subject.

'Quite a few,' my father interjected.

'Hundreds!' asserted my mother. 'What about Dunkirk?'

'Quite a few!' replied my father stoically.

Nevertheless, my mother forged ahead with her version of the *Titanic* tragedy. The ship hit an iceberg and my great uncle Bertie single-handedly rescued a great number of the unfortunate passengers.

'He shouted: "Women and children first into the lifeboats – and I'll shoot any man who disobeys me!" With this, he fired his pistol in the air.'

'Did he have to shoot anybody?' I asked. This was getting really exciting.

'Of course not – the pistol wasn't even loaded!'

'I think you'll find it was,' corrected my father.

Meetings with the great man

I remember quite clearly my meetings with the 'great man', Commander Lightoller. From the time I was about eight, on our regular trips to London's still shattered city, we would sometimes collect Grandma Gertrude from Hampstead Garden Suburb and drive her across town to Richmond to see her brother. There, while the adults talked their talk, I would sneak down to the boatyard and wander amongst the yachts, hauled up on the Hard for fitting out, anti-fouling and repainting. I've been crazy about yachts ever since.

However, sometimes I could not escape and had to face the rather daunting presence of Great Uncle Bertie and Great Aunt Sylvia. I remember the first time we drove to Richmond to meet Great Uncle Bertie. Although it was summertime, my memory of it is of a cold, wet day as we arrived by the river Thames in our not-very-up-to-date Ford. There they were – the Commander and Sylvia Lightoller. They were big and they were handsome. Great Uncle Bertie was tall and broad-shouldered, with a face still tanned the colour of leather from a lifetime at sea. Great Aunt Sylvia was younger but looked almost as tough as her husband. To me, they looked like a couple hewn from solid rock.

Great Uncle Bertie had a resonant voice with the strange indefinable accent of a mariner who has sailed the seven seas without dropping anchor anywhere for very long. I remember how, on that particular meeting, he started to regale me with tales of his maritime adventures, which included his displaying a scar on his hand that he claimed came from a shark he had harpooned and pulled onto the deck of his schooner. With relish, my great uncle described chopping the shark into sections; and how, despite this, the dismembered head gave his hand a nasty bite! My jaw dropped open. The adults laughed and I formed an impression that this was a very tough old sea dog.

The attraction of the sea

Grandma Gertrude never seemed keen to talk about her brother. Well, not until after the funeral, that is. When we left the crematorium, there was a small family gathering at the Richmond boatyard. I looked out of the window at my great uncle's motor yacht, *Sundowner*, riding to her mooring, moving gently with the tide and the windswept waves of the river. I think it was at that moment that I decided on a life at sea.

However, life doesn't always take you where you think you want to go. Much as I wanted to join the Royal Navy, I would have to wait until I was sixteen to be eligible for this; but by the time that day arrived I had already embarked upon a fledgling career in show business. Thus my seafaring days were confined to sailing small yachts around Britain's east coast. Nonetheless, I well remember the near disasters that befell my best friend and sailing companion, Ian, and myself, as we found ourselves on more than one occasion stuck on a sandbank with the tide receding and darkness coming on! Keeled over at forty-five degrees and waiting for the next tide to lift you off is no fun in the middle of the night. Ah, the follies of youth! But I have always been in love with the sea and for many years have lived close beside it, taking every opportunity to swim in or under it, as well as sailing on top of it.

As people get older, they sometimes feel a need to share things that they've kept to themselves for years. Perhaps that's why, as I was gazing out at the river and the yacht, Grandma Gertrude came up to me and said:

'What a terrible loss.'

'You mean Great Uncle Bertie?'

'Yes,' she replied, 'but also 1,535 souls lost at sea – and all unnecessarily. Dreadful things went on – and your great uncle had no control over them. Many of those involved went down with the ship; but my brother survived – and so did the man responsible... but he was disgraced and never heard of again.'

From then on, whenever I could, I spent time alone with Grandma Gertrude and plied her with questions. Slowly but surely, a picture of her brother, the adventurous 'Bertie', emerged; and it seemed as if there had been a special affection between brother and sister. She told me that in the early years together he had always referred to her as his 'chum'. Their childhood seemed full of tragedy and scandal and, perhaps to escape from this, Charles Herbert had gone off to sea at the age of thirteen, leaving Gertrude without her 'chum'.

Heroes and villains

I only asked my grandmother once why my mother's father lived in Ireland.

'There's a very good reason for that!' she snapped at me in a most uncharacteristic way. I never forgot the look on her face at that moment and I never mentioned it again. But she often spoke to me about her brother and I remember that at one point she said something that seemed quite strange:

'Most people thought my brother was a hero. Well, in a way he was; but after all – we're all human.' Then she continued, 'And there's always someone to persuade you into doing things you don't really want to do!'

This meant nothing to me at the time, although I now realise the hidden implication.

So, very early on, I realised that I had been born into a rather famous family and one full of mysteries. Mysteries that I had to wait many years to even begin to unravel.

Everyone knows the *Titanic*

So why is the world so constantly fascinated by the *Titanic*? Apparently James Cameron, in the marketing of his 1997 film of the tragedy, contended that the word *'Titanic'* was the most widely recognized proper noun in the English language after 'God' and 'Coca-Cola'! The sinking was certainly the most disastrous in maritime history prior to the First World War. There is in fact an almost endless catalogue of passenger ships lost. Even in the few early years of the twentieth century prior to the *Titanic*'s sinking there were many of these, including the *Camelot* in 1902 while en route from India to Burma with a loss of 737 lives, and the *Norge*, which lost the same number of souls when she sank in the North Atlantic in 1904. However, the 1,535 death toll on the *Titanic* eclipsed all previous passenger losses, although ships would continue to sink at an alarming rate, even in peacetime, right up to the present day. One such was the *Hans Hedtoft* which, in 1959, sank with all on board after hitting an iceberg in the North Atlantic on its maiden voyage. The vessel had been dubbed 'unsinkable'!

What then is it that so seduces and intrigues us about the sinking of what, at the time, was considered to be the most beautiful and luxurious ship ever built? Is it the apparent heroism of people like Great Uncle Bertie, swept up in a drama of huge proportions? Is it the horror of the death of what, for the privileged few, was a floating paradise? Or the tearful romance of lives sacrificed and love torn asunder?

From the moment the tragedy was announced, pens were put to paper and typewriters clattered, as writers around the world sought to cash in on this momentous event. Since then books and films, TV programmes and magazine articles have kept the name and the story of that dark event in April 1912 alive in the public eye.

Chapter 3
Titanic in the movies and on television

Cashing in on disaster

Almost from the moment the *Titanic* sank beneath the Atlantic, film producers sought to cash in on the sinking – and why not? It has all the ingredients necessary for movie success. Rich people and poor people all doomed to die together. Heroes and villains, romance and tragedy and – it is all true! What a gift to a film maker!

I love movies and it was the head teacher at my first school who was really responsible for this. He had a name that sounded as if it was straight out a Western – Seth Ward. Seth was a movie buff and every Wednesday afternoon he would show a movie. These were usually instructional but once a month we got to see a feature film. I was hooked! However, it was many years before I actually got to appear in films, and eventually write them and teach others to do so.

Although the first filmic effort after the sinking was brought out in the same year, it could hardly be called a 'movie'. It was just a quickly-cobbled-together ten-minute film, mostly showing footage of *Titanic*'s sister ship *Olympic* – to all intents and purposes, a twin of the doomed liner. Later on, I was to look more closely at this 'twin'. Moviegoers couldn't tell the two ships apart and this was certainly not an award-winning documentary. Nevertheless, it is interesting to note that *Olympic* could 'double' as *Titanic*. In the same year the Sales Company's animated version of the sinking was released, and the mind boggles at the thought of a cartoonish representation of the tragedy produced some sixteen years before Walt Disney released his first extremely simplistic Mickey Mouse short.

1912 was a busy year for movie makers anxious to cash in on the loss of more than fifteen hundred souls at sea. The Éclair Company discovered that a part-time actress, Dorothy Gibson, had actually been a *Titanic* passenger and survived the sinking. Her involvement in the disaster was dramatically enhanced to show her as a heroine of the rescue operations, something that she never claimed to be. Allegedly, the actress actually wore the same dress in the film that she had been shipwrecked in!

The Nazi *Titanic*

Surely one of the most bizarre *Titanic* films ever produced was the German attempt during World War Two to use the giant liner's sinking as a vehicle for discrediting British and American 'capitalists'. In this extraordinary 1943 film, a fictional First Officer, Herr Petersen, begs the rich and powerful owners, including the villainous owner of the ship, Bruce Ismay, to slow down. But these ruthless capitalists have wagered on setting a new speed record for the Atlantic crossing. At the Board of Trade Inquiry in Britain the White Star Line and Bruce Ismay are cleared of any fault. The blame is laid squarely on the dead Captain Smith. The epilogue to the film states: 'The deaths of 1,500 people remain unatoned, for ever a testament of Britain's endless quest for profit.'

The film was the most expensive ever made in Germany and the audiences stayed away in their droves. Joseph Goebbels, the Nazis' Head of Propaganda, had a row with the writer, Herbert Selpin, who was arrested and later found hanging in his prison cell. Not a happy production!

Nevertheless, it appears that James Cameron's script for his 1997 megahit movie has much in common with the 1943 German film.

In the 1953 *Titanic* film, Clifton Webb and Barbara Stanwyck had a Hollywood star supporting them in just about every other role in the film. This *Titanic* was shot entirely in the Twentieth Century Fox studios, but despite its lack of authenticity won an Oscar for the best screenplay.

A Night to Remember

Then in 1958 came *A Night to Remember*, regarded by many as the definitive *Titanic* film. Although much of the watery drama of passengers struggling in the freezing Atlantic was shot in Ruislip Lido, shallow enough for the 'survivors' to wade to the bank, the brilliant direction by Roy Ward Baker provided an 'on-the-spot' feel to the tragedy. The lead actor was Kenneth More, as Second Officer Lightoller; yes, my great uncle got a lead part in a movie forty-six years after the event! However, More was not well known as an actor at the time and the film was not a great financial success.

As a matter of fact, I bumped into Kenneth More – quite literally – in 1962 when he was making *The Longest Day*, the film about the Allied Forces' D-Day landings in Normandy in June 1944. He was to play a Royal Navy captain in the film and I, in one of my first West End roles, was rehearsing the part of a Russian lieutenant with an unpronounceable name in *House of Cards* at the Phoenix Theatre in London's Charing Cross Road. As I walked through the main door of Berman's, the leading film and theatre costumiers of the day, to be fitted for my nineteenth-century Russian officer's uniform, a rather short man in an expensively tailored suit and carefully arranged wavy hair collided with me as he exited through the same door.

'Terribly sorry, old boy!' he exclaimed with a beaming smile of recognition. 'And how are you, chum?'

I realised that it was Kenneth More and I knew that he'd never seen me before in his life. Somewhat flustered, I answered, 'Absolutely fine, thanks!'

'Excellent!' he sang out and, waving to me, he sprang into a waiting taxi. I stood rooted to the spot for several seconds while I tried to figure out just who the great Kenneth More thought I was. Gradually the truth dawned on me. If you're a famous film star, you work with so many people over the years that you can't possibly remember everyone, even by sight, let alone by name. Thus, the kind-hearted More, lest he offend someone he had once worked with, greeted all actors as old friends. What a charming gesture. As I went up Monty Berman's stairs in search of the nineteenth-century military department, I wondered if the great Kenneth More was even now leaning back in his taxi and wondering where he'd last worked with me – probably not. Yet another connection between me and the *Titanic*!

Actually, my great aunt, Sylvia, visited the film set of *A Night to Remember* during shooting and pronounced herself delighted with Kenneth More's performance. I find this slightly strange, as – good though he was in the part – he was a million miles away from the rough old sea dog my family all knew Great Uncle Bertie to be.

Keeping the drama alive

In *Collins Thesaurus* the word *titanic* is equated with *gigantic*, *huge*, *great*, *massive*, *towering*, *enormous*, *mighty* and *immense*. However, it also links it with *monstrous* and *elephantine*. So was the *Titanic* ship a monster? Was it too big? Was too much expected of it? I heard quite recently that several people refused to sail on the *Titanic*, regarding her as too big to survive. As ships of all sizes are referred to as 'she' and never 'it', perhaps they are more than just something made of wood or iron but are an actual 'living' thing. We humans came crawling out of the ocean all those billions of years ago, and here we are with bodies composed of up to ninety per cent water. We drink it, bathe in it, swim in it, dive under it and sail on top of it. But what about these ships that we launch upon the surface of the oceans? We build these aquatic monsters from the wood and iron of the earth and some – like the monster that Frankenstein built – can, with the help of the sea, actually destroy us. Man's inventiveness is matched only by his arrogance. Ships sail the seven seas, but many flounder and are lost. Planes fill the sky, but some fall to earth. Invention is not infallible; and so it was with SS *Titanic*. We can now marvel at the conceit and ignorance of the designers, builders, owners and crew of the *Titanic*, in their belief that this gigantic floating hotel could never come to grief. Herein lie the drama and the romance of the way in which so many of us frail humans desire to conquer the unforgiving oceans that cover so much of our planet.

A Night to Remember, and Walter Lord's excellent book of the same name on which the film was based, only served to keep the public's appetite for all things *Titanic* alive throughout the years until James Cameron delivered what many believe to be the ultimate *Titanic* movie. There have been TV films and miniseries, and even a Broadway musical, *The Unsinkable Molly Brown*, based on the 1912 disaster. In 1980 Lew Grade, the cigar-chewing British movie mogul, had a brilliant idea for a film. It was to be called *Raise the Titanic*, the story of a fictitious plan to bring the wreck to the Atlantic's surface and salvage a consignment of Byzantium, a priceless substance capable of destroying the world. The production costs are estimated to have exceeded $30 million, which was a lot of money to spend on a movie in 1980. Like the Nazis' 1943 attempt at a *Titanic* film, it lost a fortune, was universally panned by critics and deserted by audiences. The movie was Lew Grade's biggest flop and led to his classic remark:

'Raise the *Titanic*? It would have been cheaper to lower the Atlantic!'

The curse of *Titanic* strikes again? Perhaps – but definitely not for James Cameron.

Cameron hits the jackpot

When Cameron wrote, produced, directed and edited his version of *Titanic*, it was the most expensive film ever made, with an estimated final production figure of $200 million. Cameron says that when his film's budget began to expand exponentially he offered to drop all payments except his writer's fee and renounce his producer/director share of the profits. Twentieth Century Fox and Paramount, joint backers of the project, were delighted to accept his offer. Although some bones were broken and one or two actors swore never to work with Cameron again, by 1998 his had become the first film to earn more than one billion dollars at the box office, and remained the highest grossing film in cinema history until eclipsed twelve years later by *Avatar*, also written, produced, directed and edited by – yes, James Cameron. And this time, he didn't take a salary cut!

Doctor Who, the *Titanic* and me

Two great icons which never cease to fascinate those of all ages are the *Titanic* and *Doctor Who* – one an 'unsinkable' ship that got sunk, the other a man who never dies but merely morphs into another incarnation of himself. I happen to have a connection to both the ship and the Doctor. Great Uncle Bertie featured in the drama of the *Titanic*'s sinking and I featured in several episodes of *Doctor Who* in 1972. The story, with the late Jon Pertwee as the Doctor, was called *The Day of the Daleks* and was re-released in a brand-new fully digitised version in 2007 and again in 2010, resulting in a pleasant increase in my fan mail and royalties! And those Daleks – how could anyone be frightened by them? Just little guys sitting inside these tin pepperpots, pedalling them with their feet! The only thing that was frightening was the Daleks' voice: '*Exterminate! Exterminate!*' and those were laid on afterwards by a voice artist!

It certainly seems as though *Doctor Who* can literally go on for ever. The first episodes, featuring the late William Hartnell as the Doctor, were broadcast way back in 1963 and I came on the scene some nine years later. The episodes with Jon Pertwee were the first to be broadcast in colour.

Doctor Who's fascination with the *Titanic* seems almost endless, starting with Tom Baker, who followed Jon Pertwee into the role. In a story entitled *The Invasion of Time*, Tom, as the Doctor, comes across an article in the *Daily Mirror* about the great ship's sinking and is at pains to explain to a fellow Time Lord that he had absolutely nothing to do with it! That seems really strange – but then *Doctor Who* is a very strange character.

The *Titanic* crops up again when the seventh Doctor, Sylvester McCoy, is found on board the liner in one of his episodes. Not only is he on board when the liner hits an iceberg, but one of his travelling companions is accused of causing the disaster!

Christopher Eccleston, as the ninth *Doctor Who* in an episode entitled simply *Rose*, finds himself aboard the ship they said was 'unsinkable' and ends up clinging to an iceberg!

Nor should we forget Colin Baker (no relation to Tom, the fourth Doctor). Colin starred as *Doctor Who* from 1984 to 1986 and took part in an extraordinary audio production of a story entitled *The Wreck of the Titan*. In this the Doctor starts off on a voyage aboard the famous liner *Queen Mary*, which then turns into the *Titanic*, which then turns into the *Titan*! What is so extraordinary is that Morgan Robertson's novel entitled *Futility, or the Wreck of the Titan* was published in 1898 and described a giant liner, considered to be 'unsinkable', hitting an iceberg and sinking with great loss of life. Yet this was fourteen years before the *Titanic*'s maiden voyage and certainly long before J. Bruce Ismay's vision of the twin giants of the sea, *Olympic* and *Titanic*.

More recently, David Tennant's Doctor and the Australian singing star Kylie Minogue appeared together in *Voyage of the Damned*, an episode involving an interstellar space cruiser in the form of the *Titanic*. Over thirteen million British TV viewers watched this story on Christmas Day 2007; but one person was far from satisfied. Millvina Dean, the last living survivor of the sinking, complained that it was 'disrespectful to make entertainment of such a tragedy'. Perhaps she was right, but the television viewing public around the world seem to relish the strange connection between the *Titanic* and *Doctor Who* – a character who has proved, for almost fifty years, to be truly 'unsinkable'.

By the time Cameron made his version of the *Titanic* story, both Grandma Gertrude, Lightoller's sister, and his widow, Great Aunt Sylvia, were long dead. So I wonder what they would have made of one particular incident in his version of the sinking. First Officer William Murdoch, played by Ewan Stewart, is seen brandishing a pistol at the panic-stricken passengers. Lightoller does the same thing; but in the film Murdoch actually shoots two men and then turns the gun on himself – something categorically denied by my great uncle in the official inquiries held after the sinking.

Chapter 4
Bertie's adventurous life

What price progress?

In the early twentieth century great technical strides were undoubtedly made.

The first large scale production of automobiles was at the Oldsmobile factory in 1902. The Wright brothers made the first ever heavier-than-air flight in 1903. World cinema began to blossom as the new century dawned, and from 1905 the French Pathé company was producing and distributing more films worldwide than anybody else. In the US by 1907 there were four thousand Nickelodeons showing short films with piano accompaniment, while the Austrian Karl Landsteiner's research into blood types enabled the first successful blood transfusion to take place in 1907.

So, as Queen Victoria's long reign ended with her death in 1901, she left a world where Britain, Europe and the US were poised on the edge of a golden age of invention, creativity and progress. Her son who ascended to the throne as Edward VII ruled only briefly, dying in 1910; while his son, George V, and his cousin, Kaiser Wilhelm of Germany, went to war just four years later at a cost of thirty-five million lives. At much the same time, eight million are estimated to have died in the Russian revolution. Interestingly enough, King George V refused to rescue his cousin, Tsar Alexander, and his family from the revolution, leaving them to die at the hands of the

Bolsheviks: so much for family loyalty. Thus, Queen Victoria's death in fact ushered in an era of indulgence, self-interest and aggression within the ruling classes. By April 1912 the stage was set for a tragedy which, although small by comparison with the European onslaught that was to erupt just two years later, was one that would occupy writers and film-makers for generations to come.

Tragic childhood

The Lightollers were an old-established family in the Lancashire town of Chorley, where they were responsible for providing street lamps for the entire town, a charitable act well in keeping with the family motto *Lux Vestra* – 'let your light shine'.

The family story, as far as Great Uncle Bertie is concerned, is both tragic and dramatic. The children's mother died of scarlet fever shortly after Charles Herbert was born in 1874. When he was two, his father, Frederick, married again; but this wife also died some five years later when my great uncle was only seven. The double tragedy was followed by what in the nineteenth century must have been a truly shocking scandal. The story goes that in1883 one of the Lightoller maids, Joyce, gave birth to a daughter, Janet. The father, it was claimed, was Frederick Lightoller. In the light of this scandal he fled to New Zealand, taking with him his mistress, Joyce, her baby daughter and his own daughter, Gertrude's elder sister Jane, who was nineteen at the time.

The scandal hung over the deserted children, and it was during this time that Bertie and his sister Gertrude formed an especially close relationship – possibly as a defence against their uncle and aunt who, though nominally responsible for them, apparently took little interest in these children which a family scandal had so unexpectedly thrust upon them. There was therefore little resistance when young Charles Herbert, even before his fourteenth birthday, announced his desire to go to sea. His uncle must certainly have been quite pleased to be rid of the boy, for he handed over £40 as surety for the young Lightoller's Articles of Agreement, which significantly included a pledge 'to keep the Master's secrets' – a pledge that, some twenty years later, he would be held to by J. Bruce Ismay.

Grandma Gertrude, raised in the strict moral background of Victorian England, never mentioned a word of the family scandal and the painful absence of her father from her childhood. She certainly never admitted, even if she knew, that tragically he had cut his throat and died in New Zealand barely twelve months after his son, Second Officer Lightoller, survived the sinking of the *Titanic* in 1912.

Bertie never really knew his mother, and his father deserted him when he was only ten years old. Thus the tough sea captains he was to sail with would become his adoptive parents. Aboard his first ship, the *Primrose Hill*, Lightoller was accommodated with other 'young gentlemen' indentured to the vessel and its captain. In his book about my great uncle, *'Lights': The Odyssey of C. H. Lightoller*, Patrick Stenson vividly conjures up the Dickensian atmosphere of the place where the boys lived when aboard:

> But for him no roomy cabin or comfortable saloon to relax in – it was a small, evil-smelling den towards the after end of the ship, reached by descending a steep ladder leading from the fore part of the poop deck. Round its perimeter were bunks where the boys slept and in the middle a crude table with a grimy oil lamp slung above it. There were no such refinements as seats. You sat on your sea-chest.

Within a short space of time on his maiden voyage, my great uncle was exposed to the discomforts of seasickness and the terror induced by his first gale at sea. He learned that when his tutor and mentor, the Third Mate, said 'Up!' you didn't argue – you just started to climb. The *Primrose Hill* was special in that, unlike other windjammers, she carried an extra spread of sail above the rest known for obvious reasons as a 'sky' sail. These very special sails were two hundred feet above the decks.

Climbing up to attend to them was an exhausting and dangerous task. 'One hand for the ship and one hand for yourself' is a vital phrase that even an amateur yachtsman like myself quickly learns to commit to memory. In the tall ships that the young Lightoller served in, many a boy was lost when slipping from the top yardarm of a windjammer. However, Great Uncle Bertie soon learned to be fearless, a quality that would serve him well in the adventurous life to come.

Some years ago on a sea trip to Australia, I witnessed flying fish and leaping porpoises for the first time. Watching sights like this must, for the young Lightoller, have contrasted with the frightening task of working aloft when the wind blew. The young man learned, wherever possible, to steer clear of the ship's commander, Captain Anderson, if he was in one of his 'black moods' – usually induced by a lack of wind, the fuel he desperately needed to race his ship to its next destination.

First experience of ice

Great Uncle Bertie was in awe of his captain, with his rolling sailor's gait and his ability to remain master of the ship under the roughest of conditions. Although fighting remorseless gales was a terrifying experience, the young Lightoller was to discover that there was something even more threatening to the life of the ship – ice!

Aboard the *Primrose Hill*, one old mariner with a lifetime of seafaring behind him claimed to be able to 'smell' ice; and, once in an ice field, an unexpected gust of wind could easily drive a ship into the glacial arms of an iceberg.

It was a still, calm, moonless night when Lightoller first heard the old sea dog holler out, 'Ice right ahead, Sir!' But there was nothing to see – absolutely nothing to see.

Then the shout went out: 'Put your helm hard up, Sir, the ice is to windward!'

Looming out of nowhere came a great ice mountain. This is what had been stealing their wind. Slowly but surely, mindful of possible ice ledges beneath the water, the ship slipped past the iceberg and the captain decided to heave to for the night. Again, I cannot do better than quote Patrick Stenson:

> …the cold was unbearable. Everything in this ship was now frozen up; pulleys, blocks and lines solid with ice and the sails like concrete. Even the very clothes on their backs were frozen still…

When daylight came and Lightoller stepped out on deck it was to be confronted with an incredible sight: they were alongside a towering cliff of ice that seemed hundreds of feet high and stretched as far as the eye could see. They were on the edge of – Antarctica!

Storm at sea

My great uncle's second ship was *Holt Hill*, commanded by George 'Jock' Sutherland. Jock liked to drive his ships and his crew hard – too hard. Carrying twice as much canvas as a more cautious skipper would, Captain Jock pushed his luck and his ship too far. One night, Lightoller was roused from his slumbers by an almighty crashing sound, and rushing up on deck found that two of the ship's masts, complete with sails and tackle, had crashed to the deck leaving the ship to flounder. Every hand on the vessel instinctively set to with the task of making the vessel good before a strong wind could send them all to the bottom of the ocean.

Makeshift masts and sails helped the *Holt Hill* limp into Rio de Janeiro, which thankfully was only a day or two away. Unfortunately, the ship arrived in Brazil during the middle of a revolution and a smallpox epidemic. Despite this off-putting situation, the young apprentices from the *Holt Hill* stole ashore with the intention of acquiring some of the local food – preferably without paying for it. As a result, Lightoller and his friends were arrested following a fight with outraged stall holders they had attempted to rob, and were only released on an assurance from the British Consul in Rio and an undertaking from their captain.

Shipwreck

The *Holt Hill* then sailed for India via the Cape of Good Hope; but en route her captain disastrously overreached himself again, carrying too much sail in an effort to beat a rival boat. The result was the catastrophic wrecking of the ship, as the captain shouted the order no sailor wants to hear:

'Every man for himself!'

Washed back and forth by a fierce and angry sea, Lightoller jumped clear of the ship and was lucky to survive. But the loss of the ship was only part of the tragedy. Although only one man was lost in the merciless waves that beat relentlessly against an angry shore, that one man lost was Williams, the ship's mate. Tough but fair, he had become a mentor for the young apprentices and, for my great uncle, it was another father figure lost for ever while still very young. So there he was, shipwrecked on a deserted island at an age when Joseph Bruce Ismay had just started at his prep school.

A deserted island

Somehow this motley and bedraggled group of Robinson Crusoes survived. There were crayfish and vegetation to eat, but water fit to drink was discovered only at the very last moment before the men literally died of thirst. Their eventual rescuers found the *Holt Hill*'s crew weak and emaciated. However, their island was in fact quite close to Australia and Great Uncle Bertie's excitement at the wonders of the city of Adelaide helped partly to obliterate the nightmare of shipwreck and the desolate island from the young man's mind.

And so my great uncle's relationship with Australia began: a country to which he would sail often, and where his life's companion was born. Long before meeting his future wife there, the young Lightoller had fallen in love with everything about Australia – the warm days, picnics at the beach and the carefree attitude of the people.

When the Court of Marine Inquiry convened in Adelaide in 1890, George Sutherland, commander of the wrecked sailing ship *Holt Hill,* found himself tried almost as a criminal. Charged with carrying too much sail for safety, having insufficient lookouts, keeping an imperfect dead reckoning and improper log-keeping, it looked more like a trial for manslaughter or murder than a wreck enquiry. 'Jock' Sutherland's certificate as skipper was suspended for three months. Just twenty-two years later, Great Uncle Bertie would come to the defence of the ultimate commander of a sunken ship, as he framed his evidence to the *Titanic* inquiries in a fashion designed to get Joseph Bruce Ismay 'off the hook'.

As he roamed the seven seas during the twenty years previous to the *Titanic* sinking, Great Uncle Bertie suffered shipwreck more than once, endured storm, hurricane and cyclone, yet always reassured his sister, Gertrude: 'Don't you bother – the sea isn't wet enough to drown me. I'll never be drowned!'

The lure of gold

After eight years before the mast, in those beautiful but life-threatening giants of sail, Lightoller was offered his first post aboard a steam-driven vessel. His Third Mate's ticket led him to the strange and exciting world of West Africa, where unfortunately he caught malaria and was only saved by taking huge doses of quinine. It was while recuperating back in Liverpool that he heard about the rush for gold in the Klondike, that cold and inhospitable area in Canada's far north west.

The journey into this wilderness was inspired by tales brought back by prospectors who told of gold in unlimited amounts. This was enough to convince young Lightoller to make the arduous journey there. He considered himself tough and well up to the privations of gold-prospecting as, together with his friend Bill, he struggled up rocky tracks and crossed raging rivers, all with the aid of Rufus, the horse he had picked up on arrival in Canada for the challenging expedition.

Every time Lightoller hit water, which was often during this exhausting trek through unforgiving territory, he would stop to pan for the hoped-for gold. However, after weeks of fruitless search, Lightoller and Bill finally admitted that, with a chronic lack of food and the punishing weather, if they stayed in this forbidding wilderness much longer their chances of making it back to civilisation would become negligible.

Riding the range

Not wishing to return to England empty-handed, my great uncle parted from his friend Bill and rode off alone to seek his fortune – or at least three square meals a day – as a cowboy in Alberta, Canada's cattle country. With his trusty steed, Rufus, Lightoller rode the range, exchanging the rigours of fighting wind and sea for that of rounding up and wrestling steers. But in the same way that he had always longed for the sea when on dry land, Great Uncle Bertie now longed for England and home, as he tired of the North American life. However, the trip home was to be a lengthy one and the few dollars that he was offered for the faithful Rufus wouldn't get Lightoller across the two thousand odd miles to the East Coast for a ship back to England. Thus he discovered the world of the hobo, where he learned to ride a freight train without paying.

Nobody seems quite clear where the name 'hobo' comes from, but it is generally recognised as denoting someone who moves from place to place, gaining work where they can – a rootless person, yet one willing to work if the opportunity presents itself. A hobo is not a tramp – a tramp is someone who never works if he can possibly avoid it. At the bottom of the homeless pile is the 'bum', a person who will never work under any circumstances. A number of words originally particular to this travelling community became much in common use in American speech in the early and mid twentieth century. Phrases like 'the big house' for prison, 'cannonball' for a fast train and 'flop house' for an ultra-cheap hotel were becoming popular.

More cattle

Finally arriving in Montreal courtesy of the Canadian railroad system, Great Uncle Bertie, who on previous voyages had held the exalted position of Second Mate, had to take the only position available to him on a ship to Liverpool – and that was as a cattleman. Here he had to brave the stench of the animals and their spiteful frenzy at being cooped up in stalls for a long transatlantic trip. But he was going home – home to Liverpool. He had survived what he now realised had been a foolhardy adventure – the search for fame and fortune in a forbidding wilderness. The fruitless search for the prize so many men crave – gold!

Lightoller thought that his luck had changed when, once back in England and having achieved his Master's Certificate, he was offered a berth on a new steam vessel, the *Knight Bachelor* – although, when he joined the ship at Tilbury, he was only signed on as Third Mate. However, on his way to find the ship he began to sweat and shake and he recognised only too well the symptoms of a returning bout of malaria. To add to his woes, the ship he was to sail in turned out to be not the brand new *Knight Bachelor*, but the rusty old tub, the *Knight Companion*. And, worst of all – it was a cattle boat! Just the smell of the beasts and their excrement was enough to make him feel even more ill. He was in despair – he just couldn't escape from cows!

The voyage was a disaster for all concerned. Having dosed himself with quinine and somewhat recovered, he found that they were bound for Rio. But this ancient vessel was no match for the unpredictable and violent seas off the South American coast. A particularly mountainous wave almost sank the ship and carried half the cargo of live cattle over the side. When his malaria had finally abated he returned to England, vowing to be more careful about what company he sailed with in the future. The year was 1900 and his luck was finally about to change.

Chapter 5
Love, luck and
Christian Science

Marriage

Great Uncle Bertie managed to secure the position of Fourth Officer on the *Medic*, a passenger/cargo ship of the prestigious White Star Line. He found himself bound for Australia, the land that had so impressed him when, just a few years previously, he had arrived there as the survivor of a shipwreck. He loved Australia and all things Australian: which was just as well, because in 1903 something happened to unite him with Australia for ever.

On one of the *Medic*'s regular trips back to Australia from Britain, there was a young eighteen-year-old known as Sylvia Hawley-Wilson. Her full and rather exotic name was Iowa Sylvania Zillah Hawley-Wilson, something of a mouthful, so no wonder she preferred to be known as plain Sylvia. She was returning to Australia, having stayed with an aunt in England to study music and complete her education there. Her mother, Charlotte, had married an American, John Hawley-Wilson, when he came to Australia prospecting for gold. Sylvia was born at Turnkey Creek, an old mining village near the famous Abercrombie caves, some four hundred miles inland from Sydney. Unfortunately, her father was killed in a mining accident when Sylvia was very young and her mother opened a small hotel in order to support the two of them.

Sylvia was born with a club foot and so, on the trip to Australia, Lightoller took it upon himself to carry her up and down the steps of the ship whenever and wherever necessary. As the voyage progressed, so did the relationship; and by the time they arrived in Sydney, Sylvia's home town, they were definitely 'a couple'.

What is luck?

Great Uncle Bertie and Great Aunt Sylvia were married that same year in the Church of St James on King Street in Sydney, but then returned to England aboard the *Suevic*, another White Star vessel.

The newlyweds settled in Crosby, a pleasant suburb of Liverpool where some forty years earlier Joseph Bruce Ismay had been born; the man who, nine years later, would become Lightoller's nemesis, persuading our hero to risk his own reputation in order to save those of a rich man and a billion-dollar corporation.

Lightoller remained with the White Star Line, and over the next nine years rose to the rank of Second Officer on the line's *Oceanic*; thus the North Atlantic run from Liverpool to New York became a regular feature in Great Uncle Bertie's life.

On one occasion, during an American shore leave, an incident in New York changed Great Uncle Bertie's life as radically as his meeting with Sylvia on the Australia run. Someone handed him a leaflet about Christian Science, which he tucked into his pocket and later took out to study in more detail. This persuaded him to investigate further the teachings of its founder, Mary Baker Eddy.

Until this moment, Great Uncle Bertie had, as it were, taken life as it came. But as he examined the leaflet about Christian Science, he began to consider how incredibly 'lucky' he had been in his short life so far: to survive, almost unscathed, through shipwreck, storm, and dread disease, as he not only sailed the seas in often dangerous conditions, but rode the freight trains of North America as a hobo. Perhaps there was no such thing as 'luck' or even 'good fortune' for that matter. Perhaps it was his overwhelming belief in his right to survive no matter what life threw at him? Was this what had always got him through? Or was his almost unshakeable belief in his ability to survive based on some subconscious form of prayer? Had he always, unknowingly, placed his destiny in the invisible hands of a force greater than himself?

Lightoller and Christian Science

Great Uncle Bertie became a Christian Scientist just a few years before the sinking of the *Titanic* and credited his salvation from the wreck in no small part to his belief in Mary Baker Eddy's Christian Science, as exemplified by the testimony he published in the Church's *Monitor* in October 1912:

> While the *Titanic* was sinking, and during the whole time I was working at the boats, I held to the truth, thereby eliminating all fear. I was on the port side where all boats were got away without a hitch, the last one, a flat-bottomed collapsible, floating off the deck. I called on men to follow me up on top of the officers' quarters to cut adrift the last boat. We had no time to open it up, so just hove her down to the deck. I ran across the deck and could see that all material work was finished, so from where I was above the bridge, I walked into the water. The sudden immersion in this penetratingly cold water for a few seconds overcame all thought, and I struck out blindly for the crow's-nest which is on the foremast and then just above the water. I found myself drawn with great force against the grating covering the mouth of the huge forward blower. In this position I went below the surface with the ship. A doubt never entered my mind as to the ability of Divine Power to save me. These words from the ninety-first Psalm came to me so distinctly:
> 'He shall give His angels charge over thee.'

Immediately, I think, I was thrown away from the blower and came up to find a piece of wood in my hand which seemed to be attached to the top of the funnel by a wire. A second time I went down and again came to the surface. My piece of wood was gone, but alongside me was the flat-bottomed collapsible boat which I had thrown down on the other side of the ship. This I laid hold of, but made no attempt to board it. It was clear to me there was a Divine Power and it seemed perfectly natural to rely on it with the spiritual understanding spoken of in the Bible. With the sinking of a great ship like the *Titanic*, there was also the fear of suction to overcome, and at this time the forward funnel fell, throwing the boat, me, and other survivors about twenty feet clear of the ship, so that of suction we felt nothing. About thirty of us floated the remainder of the night on the upturned boat. At daybreak we found two lifeboats floating nearby, into which we were taken. Reaction or effects from the immersion were none; and though surprise has been expressed by very many, it only goes to prove that 'with God all things are possible'.

Mary Baker Eddy

Mary Baker Eddy was born in New Hampshire in 1820 and died in 1910, just two years before the sinking of the *Titanic* tested Lightoller's faith as never before. Mary was raised as a Congregationalist, a form of worship closely allied to the teachings of preachers like John Calvin, wherein the belief is that the 'Will of God' condemns some to eternal damnation and others to salvation. Mary rejected this hard-and-fast teaching quite early in her life, sensing the apparent unfairness of it. However, she developed a great interest in biblical accounts of Christ's healing powers and this was of particular importance to her, as for many years she suffered chronic illness. She was to discover that this science of healing and a devout Christian belief could work miracles for her health. The power of prayer to heal has been catalogued on countless occasions throughout the ages, but when Mary was just twelve years old she had a violent confrontation with her father over his theological beliefs in endless punishment for sinners and his daughter's sureness of God's endless love for all. This verbal battle ended with the young girl collapsing into a life-threatening fever, which thankfully prompted her father to set aside his strict moral code and join in prayer for his daughter's recovery.

In 1866, Mary had a serious fall on an icy sidewalk resulting in a spinal injury and, bedridden in great pain, she turned to her Bible and read and reread of Christ's healing powers. She could not explain how, but quite suddenly she was healed. She got up, got dressed, walked about, and from that moment on became the world's foremost advocate of Christian Science.

In 1879, finding that existing Christian churches would not accept her belief in the power of prayer to heal, Mary secured a charter to create the Church of Christ Scientist with the words: 'to commemorate the word and work of our Master, which should reinstate primitive Christianity and its lost element of healing.'

Sylvia and Christian Science

My great uncle was so impressed by Mary Baker Eddy's philosophical and scientific interpretation of Christ's teachings that he became a lifelong and devoted member of the Christian Science Movement. It made so much sense to a man who had looked death in the face on many occasions and had emerged unscathed through his firm belief that he was, in some way, being taken care of.

His lovely wife Sylvia followed her husband into the same church and remained there until her death in 1969 at the age of eighty-four. Although Great Aunt Gertrude was certainly not a follower of Christian Science, she appeared to respect her brother's belief, for I never heard her speak a disparaging word about it.

Chapter 6
Ireland, danger and scandal

My Irish grandfather

On the day of her launch, as the *Titanic* moved sedately out of Harland and Wolff's Belfast shipyard, a crowd of over a hundred thousand people lined the shores of the River Lagan to catch a sight of this magnificent sea monster, as her tugs guided her into Belfast Lough and then on to the Irish Channel and England. Among the cheering crowd were my mother, Elizabeth Hannah, then aged fifteen, together with her younger sister Eunice and their father, the Reverend William Hannah. Their mother, Grandma Gertrude, had already decamped from the family, taking with her the eldest daughter of the marriage, Theodora.

At this time, what was left of the family lived in the small fishing village of Ardglass, just a few miles from where Belfast Lough emptied into the Irish Sea. My mother recalled watching the big ships coming out into the ocean when they left the shipyard on the start of their life at sea. As well as her father and her sister, in the cheering crowds was a close friend of the Reverend Hannah's, the Ardglass harbour master, John Waters. After many years at sea, Waters was a man with an extremely observant eye who had developed a keen interest in photography.

Some thirty-three years later, my Irish grandfather and I had long talks about ships, something that I was obsessed by even at the age of six. When he mentioned the *Titanic*, I hung on his every word. The idea that he had actually seen the great ship launched impressed me hugely. It struck me as extraordinary that my mother had never mentioned being present on such an auspicious occasion.

It was only during one of our fireside chats that Grandfather Hannah recalled his friend the harbour master's phrase about the *Titanic*, as she steamed past. Looking intently through his viewfinder, he turned to my grandfather and remarked, 'There's something strange about the *Titanic*'. At the time this meant nothing to me; although, as my obsession with the *Titanic* and everything about her grew in adult life, this mysterious phrase kept coming back to me – 'something strange'. What on earth could it be?

A fishy story

Today, Ardglass is one of Northern Ireland's three major fishing ports. The harbour is much changed since the time when, as a six-year-old 'foreigner' from England, I watched huge winter waves, the height of a building, crash over the tall sea wall and run across the slippery jetty, emptying into the basin where wooden fishing boats bobbed up and down in the water.

The day's first catch of fish is now mostly exported to a variety of European destinations, but at the time of my brief stay there in 1945, fish from the boats was destined mainly for Belfast and the surrounding towns and villages. I remember watching fascinated as the local fishwives swiftly topped, tailed and gutted the fish on the harbourside trestle tables. I was all smart in my new winter coat, for my mother and I were staying with my strict grandfather, now Canon Hannah. Seeing how intrigued I was by her dexterity and speed in the beheading and gutting, one of the women invited me to try it. She handed me a fish and a small knife. As I grasped the fish to myself, all its innards tumbled out down the front of my treasured coat, leaving a stinking and unsightly mess on the closely woven tweed. The women all shrieked with laughter, as my face grew red with embarrassment. Obviously this was, as they say on TV, 'one that she had prepared earlier'.

As it happens, this was the least spectacular of my Irish adventures. World War II was still raging in Europe and, when my mother received the news that her father in Ireland was not expected to live more than a few weeks, or months at the most, she made the difficult decision to visit him before it was too late. Following Grandma Gertrude's divorce from William Hannah all those years before, she had reverted to her maiden name of Lightoller. My mother had been packed off to a boarding school in Dublin, which she hated; Theodora, being by then eighteen, opted to stay with her father and Eunice was carted off to England with her mother. Then, when my mother was seventeen, she was encouraged to come to England, although she remained locked in mourning for her lost father for the rest of her life. He, as opposed to my poor father, was the man she most admired. So, when the possibility of losing him for ever appeared, her first instinct was to hurry to him without delay.

However, as we were still a nation at war in the spring of 1945, my father was unable to leave England. Although his age prevented him from serving his country, he was nevertheless classified as a reserve required in the direst of emergencies, such as the German army actually marching up the road from Dover!

What to do with the boy

Some consideration was given, but only briefly, to leaving me in my father's care while my mother made a hasty trip for what was probably her last meeting with her father. However, my father had never learned even to boil an egg, much less look after a six-year-old boy. Although there was a possibility of billeting me on one of my father's sisters, my paternal aunts were only marginally more practical than my father. It certainly couldn't be Auntie Ethel who wore a cap and plus fours and lived with 'Auntie Bessie' who, until I was a grown man, I took to be my real aunt. Auntie Emily was stone deaf and kept chickens in a remote Buckinghamshire village. There was also another so-called aunt, known as Auntie Nellie, who lived with my great uncle Caleb, a fearsome bible-punching pig farmer in the same village.

So, eventually the decision was made – I would accompany my mother to Ireland across the sea and my father would move in with one or other of his strangely unorthodox relatives.

A perilous crossing

The shortest sea crossing from the British mainland to Northern Ireland is from Stranraer in Scotland to Larne, north of Belfast, a distance of about twenty-five nautical miles. Although this route entailed my mother and me travelling almost four hundred miles by train to reach our point of embarkation on the wild west coast of Scotland, this was the shortest journey possible through waters still regularly patrolled by packs of enemy U-boats.

How my mother felt about taking her only child on this brief but perilous sea journey I have no idea, but I imagine that the opportunity to see her father after so long an absence and before his likely death must have outweighed any fears for our safety. Although the end of World War II was only a few months away, numerous German submarines still lurked beneath the waters of the Irish Sea, as Britain's shipping passed through this narrow channel from Liverpool en route for the North Atlantic. In fact, during the first few months of 1945, as many as ten German U-boats were either sunk or captured, which gives some indication of the size of the menace that still lurked there.

And so it was that I found myself in mid winter in the last months of World War II on a small ship that had a very real possibility of ending as a tasty snack for a roving sea-wolf.

Emergency – U-boat!

As it happened, the ship must have received a U-boat warning, for halfway across the Irish Channel we were all ordered to don life jackets. Finding a steward busily tugging piles of these from a cupboard, I asked – in typical precocious fashion – if I could help.

'Okay,' he said, 'you can hand some of these out,' and thrust a couple into my arms. What excitement! What a responsible task for a boy of six! I spent the next ten minutes or so happily rushing backwards and forwards to and from the life jacket cupboard, collecting a couple at a time and thrusting them into the arms of various surprised passengers.

Passengers in danger

And so, almost thirty-three years after life jackets were handed out to passengers on the doomed *Titanic*, I was handing out the same kind of life-preservers to travellers also in dire danger on the sea, and only a few nautical miles from the Belfast shipyard where the *Titanic* had been prepared for her first and last voyage.

Of course, my mother and I managed to cross the narrow straits between Scotland and the Northern Irish coast without mishap. However, this famous funnel of water has claimed many lives over the years.

In January 1953, the car ferry *Princess Victoria*, caught in a severe windstorm, sank with the loss of 133 lives off the Irish coast near the fishing village of Ardglass, where I had stayed with Grandfather Hannah in 1945. It was Britain's worst maritime disaster since World War II.

My grandfather, William Hannah, was connected in more ways than one with the strange case of the *Titanic*. I obviously knew that, if he married into the Lightoller family, he must in some way be related to my famous great uncle, Commander Lightoller.

Another family scandal

In the early part of the twentieth century, the Reverend William Hannah had already been rector of the parish of Ardglass for a number of years. Later he would become Canon of Downpatrick Cathedral, the abbey that served all of County Down.

Some ten years after her husband's death, Great Aunt Sylvia revealed to me the scandal that had prevented William Hannah from taking his rightful place as an Archbishop of the Church. I was sitting with her on the deck of the motor yacht, *Sundowner*, at her mooring by the slipway that led down to the water from the Lightoller boatyard. This was now run by her son as, at seventy-seven, my great aunt was no longer of an age to take charge of it, although she certainly retained an active interest. I remember that it was a warm summer's day, as our conversation turned to her sister-in-law, Grandma Gertrude.

'A bit mad,' was my great aunt's opinion of her. Personally, I think I would have used the word 'eccentric'. She continued, 'You certainly can't blame her for what happened.'

When I queried this remark, she went on: 'You know why she divorced Hannah and left Ireland, don't you?' I had absolutely no idea, so Great Aunt Sylvia wasted no time in telling me.

'Your Grandfather Hannah was rather overfond of the choirboys in his church.'

To say that this was a revelation is an understatement. My mother had always held her father up as a shining example of a 'Man of God'. Of course, many a so-called 'Man of God' has been found to have sexual proclivities not necessarily in line with the prescribed moral code of the day. I had no reason to disbelieve my great aunt, but it was hard to reconcile the thought of my maternal grandfather in this light with the man who had so impressed me by his dignity and humour as a six-year-old boy. However, there were further family revelations to come. According to Great Aunt Sylvia, my dear old dad, Henry Palmer, was not my mother's first husband!

'She just used him to get out of an unhappy first marriage.'

Sylvia Lightoller was now well into her stride. I waited to discover if she was going to dig out any more skeletons from the family cupboard.

'What did your grandmother tell you about the Commander?' she asked.

'That everybody thought he was a hero,' I replied.

'So he was,' she said. 'But it's not always easy to remain a hero day after day under any circumstances.'

Abruptly, the conversation turned to another subject – my recent trip to Australia – and we were able to find much to talk about. Quite obviously, both the Lightoller and Palmer sides of the family had many secrets to hide. Certainly this conversation with my great aunt reawakened in me a strong desire to get to the bottom of the whole Lightoller/*Titanic* mystery.

Lightoller's place in the scheme of things

Britain has always been ruled by, and fascinated by, 'Class' with a capital C. By the beginning of the twentieth century, agricultural workers and smallholders had largely disappeared into what William Blake called 'the dark, satanic mills' of the Industrial Revolution. Steam was the power, and steel was the material that not only created fortunes for Britain's mill owners but built the giant ships of the White Star Line, into whose service my great uncle entered in 1900. By this time he had spent some twenty-six years at sea, mainly in giant sailing ships. He was therefore, by the start of the new century, a seasoned mariner having, as he delighted in telling me, been shipwrecked several times, cast away on a deserted island and nearly died of malaria.

Despite his swashbuckling nature, Lightoller was only too aware of his station in life. Prior to the American investigation into the *Titanic*'s sinking, Lightoller had several private meetings with J. Bruce Ismay, owner of the White Star Line, who appears to have made clear to him exactly where his loyalties should lie. A brave, tough, straight-talking man, Great Uncle Bertie was also what my grandmother described as a 'company man'. For this reason there are those who believe that, during both the American and British inquiries, he may have 'bent the truth' on several occasions, in order to save the good name of the company, its owner and the officers lost in the sinking.

In fact, according to witnesses of the time, some of his testimonies may have indeed saved the company from bankruptcy and liquidation. In his autobiography, *Titanic and Other Ships*, Lightoller admits to being part of a White Star 'whitewash': something corroborated by my second cousin, Lady Louise Patten, in the afterword to her excellent book *Good as Gold*, as she had gained first-hand accounts of the 'whitewash' from both her mother and her grandmother, Sylvia Lightoller, my great aunt. Great Uncle Bertie comments in his book that:

> At the inquiry in London it was very necessary to keep one's hand on the 'whitewash brush'. Sharp questions that needed clever answers, if one was to avoid a pitfall carefully, subtly dug, leading to a pinning down of blame onto someone's luckless shoulders. I think in the end the White Star Line won.

In her book my second cousin Louise quotes the above passage and adds a brief but telling comment to the whole sorry business. 'As the past century has shown, White Star's cover-up did indeed succeed and the truth was lost.'

Part Two
Survivors and
Courtroom Dramas

Chapter 7
The White Star Line and Lightoller

The appeal of Titanic

Why the lasting appeal of the *Titanic*? Well, we have seen that its sinking was symbolic of the end of an era. A ship laden with selfish, moneyed people goes down – but also with the poorest 'steerage' passengers sharing the same fate. In extreme situations 'Class' disappears and only bravery and cowardice, panic and calmness are present. Astor's millions were of no use to him as the waves closed over his head. Ismay jumped into a lifeboat full of women and children. Disaster is the great leveller.

As audiences watch the *Titanic* movies and devour *Titanic* books, what is it that is so gripping? They know the outcome – the ship will sink, fifteen hundred or more lives will be lost. The end of the drama is known before it begins. Is it the attraction of 'What would I have done?' Or is it a fly-on-the-wall view of good and bad under extreme circumstances? I choose to think that, although it may be both these, it is also the idea of the 'unsinkable' sinking. Our worst nightmare, if you like. Why do people enjoy horror films? Perhaps because it is a nightmare that they know they can wake from. Those on the *Titanic* lived inside a nightmare from which there was no escape; witnessing this at second hand gives us pause to think of the blessings that we enjoy – our job, our family and our friends. 'There, but for the grace of God, go I.'

So, how am I to arrive at the truth of the *Titanic*'s sinking and Great Uncle Bertie's involvement in it? Well, perhaps the only course is to follow the official American and British inquiries. What did the survivors who were called as witnesses tell us of the monstrous event? Did their stories conflict? Did officialdom want to sweep the terrible incident under the carpet? We should remember that both British and American national pride and reputation were at stake when it came to the official inquiries on both sides of the Atlantic.

The Ismays

Thomas Ismay, J. Bruce Ismay's father, acquired the White Star Line in 1868 and soon after agreed a deal with the owners of the Irish shipbuilding yard of Harland and Wolff. The agreement was that, for a consideration, the Belfast shipbuilders would not build for any of White Star's rivals.

It has long been a tradition with certain shipping lines to have a common theme running through the name of all their ships. In the case of White Star this was that their vessels' names all ended in -*ic*. However, the company suffered a setback when, in 1873, the year before my great uncle was born, the White Star's prize ship SS *Atlantic* sank off the coast of Canada with the loss of 535 lives. The subsequent Canadian inquiry blamed the crew for poor navigation, while the British Board of Trade cleared the company of any wrongdoing: a finding similar to the Board's recommendation at the *Titanic* inquiry some thirty-nine years later. So – nothing new there then!

However, the curse of -*ic* continued. In 1893 the *Nordic* vanished in the Atlantic. Neither she nor her seventy-four passengers and crew were ever found. Then, in 1907, *Servic* ran aground off England's south-west coast. Miraculously all her 456 passengers and forty-one crew were saved. However, two years later the *Republic* collided with an Italian liner off

Newfoundland and sank with four lives lost. In September 1911, just months before the launching of the *Titanic*, her sister ship *Olympic* collided with a warship in the Solent, badly damaging both craft. You really would think that Thomas' son, J. Bruce Ismay, by now Managing Director and Chairman of White Star, would have got the message. No, the *Titanic* became yet another ill fated *-ic* vessel. However, the subsequent loss at sea of the *Arabic*, the *Britannic*, the *Cymric*, the *Launtic*, the *Afric*, the *Delphic* and the *Laurentic* over the following years failed to dissuade the White Star Line from choosing *-ic* when it came to naming ships!

Thomas Ismay was, by all accounts, an overbearing father and autocratic employer. Frances Wilson, in her fascinating book *How to Survive the Titanic, or the Sinking of J. Bruce Ismay*, says that Bruce Ismay's father regarded him as a 'mother's boy'... However, the *Boston Globe* described Bruce as 'one of the best dressed men in England', so at least he was a natty dresser. But he was also described as 'a bit of a loner', possibly a misanthropist – he just didn't like people that much. No doubt Bruce Ismay, finding himself as owner and manager of the prestigious White Star Line on his father's death, sought to emulate the dynamic and demanding Thomas in his relationship with those who worked for him. This included the *Titanic*'s Second Officer, Charles Herbert Lightoller.

Ismay and the tennis champ

One hundred years ago, J. Bruce Ismay would have been considered extremely tall, at six feet four inches. He had acquired the reputation of being a loner and, although a keen sportsman, was not a team player, being particularly good at tennis. His stand-offish nature was no doubt cultivated to counteract the regular lambasting from his rather cruel and supercilious father, Thomas Ismay. There seems little doubt that Bruce Ismay enjoyed his position as some kind of celebrity aboard the *Titanic*, being the perceived owner of the White Star Line. He dined with a number of First Class passengers and it is likely that among them was Karl Behr, a top tennis player who had been a finalist at Wimbledon in 1907.

Behr and Helen Newson would become immortalised in their granddaughter Helen Behr Sanford's romance, *Starboard at Midnight*. This book retells the story of Behr boarding the *Titanic* for its doomed voyage in the hopes of persuading the beautiful Helen to marry him. The couple survived but Behr always suffered, like many of the men who made it into the lifeboats, with extreme feelings of guilt that he had reached safety when so many others of the male passengers had not.

Lightoller and his nemesis

Joseph Bruce Ismay was twenty-two years older than Charles Herbert Lightoller. Although Ismay was 'new money' he was hugely rich and to all intents and purposes was the boss of the White Star Line, a long and illustrious line of steam ships swallowed up by J. P. Morgan's International Maritime Marine company (IMM). Certainly there were things in common between Ismay and Morgan. They were both the taciturn sons of successful fathers and devoted to the acquisition of riches. John Pierpont Morgan's motto was 'Think a lot, say little, and write nothing'!

So, while the White Star continued to fly under a British flag with British crews, it was nevertheless from now on definitely American.

J. P. Morgan thought he was doing the British a great favour, because the money he paid for the White Star Line was well above the going rate, and the British shareholders benefited hugely from this. However, Britons like to keep things British and so, when Morgan visited London shortly after the acquisition, society did not throw open its doors to him in quite the way he expected.

By the time he joined the White Star Line in 1901, at the age of thirty-three, Great Uncle Bertie had already had an extremely tough life. On the other hand, Bruce Ismay's life had also been tough but in other ways. Not only did Bruce receive no affection as a child from his father, but at both his posh prep school and later at Harrow he was unable to relate to other boys, and remained a stiff, aloof character all his life.

The rescue ship reaches New York

As the *Carpathia* docked at New York's Pier 54 on April 18th 1912, the press crowded the wharf to view the survivors and Captain Rostron, the *Carpathia*'s Chief Officer, posed for photographs. On arrival in New York, all those who had survived the *Titanic*'s sinking were served with warrants to prevent them leaving America before being called to give evidence to the hastily convened Senate Inquiry into the disaster. Lightoller and Ismay were among those quickly whisked away, to be hidden from the glare of press scrutiny and public gaze alike. They were kept under close watch while waiting for the inquiry to begin, making it impossible for the two men to continue the intimate conversations that they had held together while travelling to New York on the *Carpathia*: conversations that very likely covered, in great detail, every aspect of the sinking of the *Titanic*.

From the guarded nature of some of Lightoller's answers to the Senate Inquiry, and his subsequent admission that he had on more than one occasion been somewhat conservative with the truth, it seems very possible that during their time together on the *Carpathia*, Ismay had made Lightoller 'an offer he couldn't refuse'.

If I were writing a film about Great Uncle Bertie's involvement with the *Titanic*, I would probably not start with the launch, the cruise and the sinking, in the way *A Night to Remember* and various other good accounts do. I would open on something truly dramatic, like the *Carpathia* landing survivors in New York and the Senate Inquiry that followed. It wasn't exactly a trial as such, for no one was accused of any crime. However, the proceedings did have all the ingredients of a courtroom drama. 1,535 people had lost their lives and the two men who might have had something really important to say, Captain Smith and First Officer Murdoch, were dead and buried deep beneath the sea. The most senior surviving officer, Charles Herbert Lightoller, and the man who ran the White Star Line, Joseph Bruce Ismay, would surely be able to explain not only why the *Titanic* hit an iceberg, but also why so many unfortunate souls lost their lives that fateful night. However, Lightoller and Ismay shared secrets they were not going to reveal to either the US Senate Inquiry or its equivalent in London.

A view from the press

The headline splashed across the front page of the *New York American* newspaper on Wednesday April 17th 1912 read:

ALL TITANIC SAVED IN CARPATHIA
No Hope Left: 1,535 Dead

This headline was composed in such a way as to be easily misread by someone giving only a cursory glance at the paper. At first sight it looked as though everyone had been rescued by the *Carpathia*. Only on slightly closer inspection would the full enormity of the event strike home. Beneath the headline at least half the page was taken up with a photograph of a ship's deck entirely surrounded by a sea of floating ice. The caption beneath the picture read:

> The French liner, *Niagara*, which arrived yesterday, hit two small nearly submerged icebergs last Friday night, which crushed her starboard bow. She called for aid by wireless. The Cunarda *Carmania* responded and stood by until the *Niagara*'s captain found his ship able to proceed unassisted. The photograph above was taken at daylight after the accident.

The *Niagara* appeared to have been far luckier than the ill-fated *Titanic*. Or was it luck? If the *Titanic* had struck an iceberg in the same way the *Niagara* had, with her bows, usually the toughest part of a ship, rather than scraping her side, acknowledged to be the weakest part of a vessel, the tragedy and huge loss of life might have been avoided. The reasons for the way in which the *Titanic* hit the iceberg would only be partly revealed in the official inquiries.

The rest of the first page of the *New York American* newspaper was taken up with a list of the *Titanic*'s rescued and missing. It was continued on page four of the paper and commenced with '1st Class Passengers known to be aboard the *Carpathia*, followed by the other names plus those believed to have perished.'

Lastly, the paper's front page carried an article sent by telegraph from SS *Bruce* en route to Sydney, a report that does not easily match later testimonies heard in the inquiries. For instance, the paper quotes that: 'The impact almost rent the ship asunder.' In fact, experts later claimed that had the *Titanic* remained stationary, instead of proceeding under way again, at Bruce Ismay's instruction, the ship might not have sunk before help reached her. 'Passing over the submerged portion of the iceberg, it is supposed to have torn the bottom out of the liner,' is another likely inaccuracy.

On the morning of April 15th the White Star offices in Liverpool had been besieged by both the press and anxious relations of those on board the *Titanic*. Company officials were so fearful for their safety that they addressed the crowds with updates of the situation from balconies high up in the building.

Back in New York, the survivors all had stories to tell and, like the packs of avaricious paparazzi of today, the early twentieth-century press couldn't wait to pounce on these poor people to extract suitable titbits of tragedy to feed to their eager readers. Gradually the awful truth dawned on an unsuspecting world. The biggest, grandest and most desirable floating hotel ever built had gone down with almost seventy per cent of its passengers and crew.

Chapter 8
Survivors and their stories

'The black family'

From the survivors there were tales of tragedy, bravery, ill luck and good fortune. For instance, there was only one black person aboard the ship, but he had not survived the sinking. Joseph Laroche was in fact originally from the Caribbean island of Haiti, but had spent the last eleven years of his life in France, where he married four years before embarking in the *Titanic* at Cherbourg. His wife Juliette and their two little daughters were also on the voyage and survived the sinking. Juliette died in 1980 at the age of ninety-one; but what is so striking about this family's sad story is that there is no record of anyone ever mentioning a 'black family' aboard the *Titanic*: not from fellow passengers, crew nor in any of the press coverage of the disaster. This is quite unusual, as racial prejudice was very much in evidence in both the US and Britain a hundred years ago.

Kidnapped

Then there is the story of two small children kidnapped by their father, a French tailor named Michel Navratil, separated from his wife Marcelle pending a divorce. Fearful of losing his children, the Frenchman chose to snatch them when they were on a visit to him, carrying them off in the *Titanic* under the assumed name of Hoffman. Once the ship sailed, 'Hoffman' kept himself and his two little boys – Michel, aged three, and Edmond, two – confined to his cabin. Their father perished in the disaster but not before handing his two young sons into the arms of those escaping in Lifeboat D.

Aboard the rescue ship *Carpathia*, the two youngsters, unable to speak any English, became known as 'the orphans of the *Titanic*' when nobody came forward to claim them after the tragedy. However, the children's mother, Marcelle, read about the 'orphans' and, having by then traced her errant husband's escape route, was able to claim the children to the satisfaction of the White Star Line. The company gave her a free ticket on the *Oceanic* to New York, where she was reunited with her little boys on May 16th 1912. Michel, the elder of the two boys by one year, died in France in January 2001 – the last male survivor of the sinking.

Jack Thayer's story

John B. Thayer, a prominent official of the Pennsylvania Railroad Company, was lost in the *Titanic*'s sinking; but his wife Marian – the object of J. Bruce Ismay's unrequited love – survived together with their seventeen-year-old son, Jack.

During the night of April 14th, Jack noticed that he could no longer feel air streaming in through the half-open porthole of his First Class cabin. He could not later recall any sensation of a collision but, sensing that the ship had stopped, he dressed and went up on deck. Walking towards the bow, he could see ice on the forward well deck. Jack then woke his parents, who went up on deck with him and, noticing that the ship was developing a list to port, they returned to their rooms to put on warmer clothes and life jackets. They returned to the deck once more, but somehow Jack lost sight of them and, after searching for some time, he assumed his parents had boarded a lifeboat.

Eventually, as the ship was actually sinking, Jack jumped into the water. He managed to reach the overturned collapsible lifeboat that Great Uncle Bertie had unsuccessfully attempted to launch and on which he and a number of other men were now standing in a most precarious fashion. After spending the night standing on the overturned collapsible, Jack was picked up by Lifeboat 12, little realising that his mother was in nearby Lifeboat 4. Nor did she realise her son was saved until they were reunited on the *Carpathia*.

Some twenty-eight years later, Jack decided to write an account of his experience on the terrible night:

> There was peace and the world had an even tenor to its way. Nothing was revealed in the morning the trend of which was not known the night before. It seems to me that the disaster about to occur was the event that not only made the world rub its eyes and awake but woke it with a start keeping it moving at a rapidly accelerating pace ever since with less and less peace, satisfaction and happiness. To my mind the world of today awoke April 15th 1912.

Tragedy dogged Jack Thayer throughout his life. Having lost his father in the 1912 wreck, his son Edward was killed on active service in 1945 near the end of World War II. The lasting trauma of the *Titanic*'s sinking plus the loss of his son led Jack to take his own life in the same year. His mother, the once vivacious Marian Thayer, loved by J. Bruce Ismay from afar, had died the previous year. Her death occurred on April 14th 1944, exactly thirty-two years to the day after the *Titanic* began to sink, taking her husband, John, with it.

The austere and aloof Bruce Ismay appears to have been wildly infatuated with Marian Thayer, with whom he kept up an intimate correspondence for many years after the tragic sinking. Although he may have considered this to be for him a case of unrequited love, Marian never saw their arm's-length relationship as anything other than platonic.

Romance

For the past one hundred years since the sinking, the public at large have been fascinated not only by the causes of the

Titanic's demise, but also by the tales of romance involving some of the survivors.

Robert Daniel from Philadelphia met fellow survivor Mary Eloise Smith on the *Carpathia*, her husband Lucien having been lost when the *Titanic* went down. They became close friends and two years later were married.

Daniel and Mary Marvin were returning to New York on the *Titanic* after honeymooning in Europe. Although Daniel was lost in the sinking, six months later Mary gave birth to a daughter, Mary Margaret. However, happiness was to follow tragedy when Daniel's widow fell in love with Howard de Camp who, in 1916, adopted little Mary Margaret as his own daughter.

'The Unsinkable Molly Brown'

'The Unsinkable Molly Brown' was only ever known in real life as Margaret, the 'unsinkable' title having been bestowed upon her by the writers of a Broadway musical and the follow-up Hollywood film based on her life and exploits, including her extrovert personality and bravery during the sinking of the *Titanic*.

Born in Missouri in 1867, Margaret Brown, as she became by marriage, was a declared feminist. She belonged to the National American Women's Association, ran soup kitchens for the needy and raised the money required for the building of a new hospital. Well off through her husband's successful gold-mining, Margaret Brown was an unstoppable force, entering high society with a flagrant disregard for the disapproval her extrovert personality caused among the 'ladies who lunch'.

While on a trip to France, Margaret Brown heard that one of her grandchildren was sick and hurriedly booked the first passage she could get back to the US. This was on the ill-fated *Titanic* and, as the ship sank, she exhorted the women in Lifeboat Number 6 to 'Row, ladies, row!' She subsequently raised ten thousand dollars for the desperate survivors of the sinking. The equivalent of this sum today would probably be closer to three hundred thousand dollars. For this and other philanthropic deeds she was awarded the French *Légion d'Honneur*. Although it was Broadway that gave her the name 'unsinkable', it was surely a most apposite description of Margaret Brown.

In America immediately after the disaster a number of other charities were set up to bring aid to the survivors, most of whom had lost all of their belongings in the sinking and would soon discover that the White Star Line had no intention of paying them compensation of any kind. On April 29th 1912, the great Caruso and members of the Metropolitan Opera raised twelve thousand dollars for those who had suffered in the disaster. At today's rates this is probably close to three hundred and sixty thousand dollars. Back in Southampton, where so many of the ship's crew had come from, it was claimed that over a thousand local families had been directly affected.

The Waldorf-Astoria

The initial Senate Inquiry was held in the magnificent Waldorf-Astoria hotel in Park Avenue, New York, commencing on April 19th 1912 and moving the following week to the Russell Senate Building in Washington DC. The Waldorf-Astoria was originally conceived as two separate hotels; the first, named the Waldorf, was built in 1893 at the behest of William Waldorf-Astor. The second was built for his cousin John Jacob Astor IV and he called it the Astoria. The two buildings were closely adjacent and were shortly connected by a passageway. Thus was born the hyphenated Waldorf-Astoria.

By an unhappy coincidence, John Jacob Astor IV, creator of the Astoria part of the conjoined hotels, died in the *Titanic*'s sinking. This was a man of astonishing inherited wealth who was also gifted as an inventor and writer. Added to this he was an army colonel and successful real-estate developer. However, in 1909, when he was forty-four, he divorced his wife in order to marry a young woman of eighteen, Madeleine Talmage Force. American society was scandalised as, apart from anything else, the new bride was younger than John Jacob's own son.

The couple fled abroad, hoping that in time the whole thing would blow over. However, in Europe, as in the US, the couple were shunned by their fellow Americans, with one notable exception: Margaret Brown – the 'Unsinkable Molly Brown'. She befriended the couple, travelling together with them to Egypt and France. It was pure coincidence that the three of them embarked on the ill-fated maiden voyage of the *Titanic*, as Madeleine Astor was by now heavily pregnant and wanted her baby born in America.

As the *Titanic* was sinking, my great uncle attempted to adhere strictly to the principle of 'women and children first'. Thus, when Astor asked to accompany his pregnant wife in a lifeboat, describing her condition as very 'delicate', Lightoller refused. The last that the young Madeleine Astor saw of her husband, as the lifeboat was lowered to the water, was his figure on the boat deck nonchalantly smoking a cigarette and chatting to a friend. So, in his attempt to stick to the rules, Second Officer Lightoller deprived a pregnant young wife of a husband, a baby about to be born of a father and the world of a remarkable and gifted man.

Who are the bad guys?

So now the stage was set for a courtroom-style drama where the apparent bad guy, Ismay, may or may not have coerced the apparent good guy, Lightoller, into bending his testimony. If the White Star Line was found to be at fault, if it could have avoided the sinking, then their insurance for the loss could be declared null and void. The resultant bankruptcy would not be the first for White Star, as it had also faced this possibility in October 1867. At that time, the White Star Line concentrated on a Liverpool to New York service, with heavy investment in new ships financed by borrowing. However, in 1867 the company's bank, the Royal Bank of Liverpool, failed and White Star was left with an outstanding debt of five hundred and twenty-seven thousand pounds (almost thirty-five million pounds today).

As Grandma Gertrude indicated to me, few heroes are ever completely good or villains completely bad: 'Sometimes you may be forced to bend the truth a little to save the many.'

The collapse of the White Star Line in 1912 would have meant the loss of Great Uncle Bertie's job and he had a large house and servants to maintain, not to mention a wife and five children! It would also mean no more jobs for any of his shipmates who had sailed and survived with him.

Chapter 9
Let the trial begin

The basic facts

These are the basic facts as presented to the US inquiry:

On April 10th *Titanic* left Southampton on England's south coast for her maiden voyage. She carried 1,316 passengers; these included multimillionaires like John Jacob Astor IV (who joined at Cherbourg) and Benjamin Guggenheim, together with 706 Third Class passengers as 'steerage'. (No one seems quite sure where the term 'steerage' came from. Possibly it was because cattle (steers) were often transported far below decks in merchant steamers, but it also may have been because the steering gear from helm to rudder ran through the 'below-decks' accommodation where Third Class passengers were often carried.)

By Sunday April 14th, *Titanic* was approaching a speed of 21.5 knots – approximately twenty-five miles per hour – and it appears that she was still steaming at this speed when she entered the ice fields.

At 11.40pm Frederick Fleet on lookout in the crow's nest noted something in the distance, but his warning to the bridge apparently came too late to avoid the collision. At 2.20am, just two hours and forty minutes after striking the iceberg, the *Titanic* broke in two (according to some survivors) and sank with the loss of 1,535 lives. It was not until almost two hours later that the *Carpathia* arrived at the scene of the disaster.

Warning! Ice!

At this point it may be helpful to review the numerous warnings of ice received by *Titanic* prior to her sinking. It seems quite extraordinary that the ship would continue at almost her maximum speed into an ice field despite these warnings.

On the evening of April 13th the *Titanic* received a signal from the *Rappahanock* saying that she had sustained damage passing through an ice field. At nine o'clock the next morning a wireless message from *Caronia* warned of icebergs at 42 degrees north and between 49 and 51 degrees west. Later that morning, many of the passengers attended morning service, which was substituted for the proposed lifeboat drill. While they were emerging from the service, the Dutch liner *Noordam* reported 'much ice' in the same position as the *Caronia* had.

Shortly after lunch on April 14th, iceberg warnings were received from the *Baltic* at latitude 41 degrees north, longitude 49 degrees west, stating large quantities of field ice. This meant that it was about 150 miles dead ahead of the *Titanic.* The message was delivered to Captain Smith who passed it to Ismay, but he just put it in his pocket, later displaying it to two lady passengers, thus delaying vital information reaching the relevant officers. A few minutes later, there was a warning from the German liner *Amerika* of a large iceberg at 41 degrees north, 50 degrees west; but this message was never sent to the bridge. For some reason, Captain Smith altered the ship's course to the south and west of the normal course. Perhaps this was to avoid ice, although if so it certainly did not work.

At 7.30 in the evening of April 14th, three messages about large icebergs were picked up from the *Californian* at 42 degrees north, 49 degrees west. The messages were delivered to First Officer Murdoch on the bridge. Captain Smith was busily engaged at a dinner party, although ice was now only fifty miles ahead. At five to nine that evening, Captain Smith left the dinner party, went to the bridge and had a lengthy discussion with Second Officer Lightoller, who by now had taken over the watch from Murdoch. They had a discussion about visibility and icebergs and, when Captain Smith retired for the night at 9.20, Lightoller sent repeated messages to the crow's nest to keep a careful watch out for icebergs. However, ten minutes later the *Mesaba* sent warning of an iceberg at latitude 42 to 41 north, longtitude 49 to 50 west, but this was overlooked because the operators were too busy sending and receiving personal messages for passengers.

Altogether there were six warnings that day, indicating a huge field of ice about seventy-eight miles long and directly ahead of the *Titanic*. In other words, the Captain of the *Titanic* and his officers should have known full well that they were endangering the lives of their passengers, the crew and the ship herself by continuing on that course at that speed. Added to which, a ship with a length of almost nine hundred feet and a weight of forty-six thousand tons was not an object that could drastically change course in a dire emergency such as the approach of a giant iceberg.

Corporate-speak!

J. Bruce Ismay was the first person called before the US Senate Inquiry into the sinking of the *Titanic*. Having confirmed his name, age, place of residence and position as managing director of the White Star Line, he announced: 'In the first place I would like to express my sincere grief at this deplorable catastrophe.'

He then grasped the opportunity to address the committee in a manner that reads more like a man reporting to his company's shareholders than one whose arrogance and foolhardiness may have directly or indirectly caused the death of over fifteen hundred people: 'I understand that you gentlemen have been appointed as a Committee of the Senate to inquire into the circumstances.'

Ismay then went straight into 'corporate' mode, using 'we' rather than 'I'.

So far as we are concerned, we welcome it – we want the fullest inquiry. We have nothing to conceal – nothing to hide. The ship was built in Belfast. She was the latest thing in the art of shipbuilding. Absolutely no money was spared in her construction. She underwent her trials which were entirely satisfactory.

Asked by Senator Smith to describe the trials the ship went through, Ismay was forced to admit that he was not present for these. In fact, as no senior representative of the company was aboard the *Titanic* for these trials, one must wonder how he deduced that they were entirely satisfactory. However, Ismay continued with his own version of events:

She arrived at Southampton on Wednesday 3rd I think and sailed on Wednesday 10th leaving at twelve o'clock. She arrived in Cherbourg that evening having run at 68 revolutions. We left Cherbourg and proceeded to Queenstown (Ireland). We arrived there at about midday on Thursday. We ran at 70 revolutions. The second day the number of revolutions was increased to about 72 revolutions. On that second day I think we ran 519 miles.

This suggests an average speed over a twenty-four-hour period of about 18.5 knots (21.6 miles per hour).

The second day we ran 549 miles. The weather during this time was absolutely fine, with the exception, I think of about ten minutes' fog one evening. I understand that it has been stated that the ship was going at full speed. The ship never had been at full speed. The full speed of the ship is 78 revolutions. So far as I am aware she never exceeded 75 revolutions. It was our intention, if we had fine weather on Monday afternoon or Tuesday, to drive the ship at full speed. That, owing to the unfortunate catastrophe, never eventuated. The accident took place on Sunday night, what exact time it was, I don't know. I was in bed myself, asleep when the accident happened. The ship sank, I am told, at 2.20am.

Ismay declared that, donning his coat, he went up to the bridge and asked Captain Smith what had happened. The Captain replied that the ship had struck ice and was seriously damaged. Going below again, Ismay accosted Bell, the Chief Engineer, who confirmed what the Captain had said, adding that he was confident the pumps would keep the ship afloat. Back on deck, Ismay heard the order given to 'Get the boats out!'

He told the inquiry that he then 'walked along the starboard side of the ship, where I met one of the officers. I told him to get the boats out...'

'What officer?' interjected Senator Smith.

'That I could not remember, sir,' replied Ismay, and then went on: 'I stood on the deck practically until I left the ship in the starboard collapsible boat which was the last boat to leave the ship, as far as I know.'

Here his implication was clearly that he was the last, or one of the last, to leave the ship, which – from reports of him leaping into a boat reserved for women and children – was manifestly untrue.

Senator Smith then asked: 'Did the officers seem to know the seriousness of the collision?'

'That I could not tell, sir, because I had no conversation with them.'

'Go to Hell!'

Fifth Officer Lowe considered that by continually shouting out 'Lower away, lower away, lower away!' Ismay was being unhelpful, and actually interfering; so he told Ismay 'to get the hell out of it' and let him get on with what he was doing.

Although this may seem like downright insubordination, given the circumstances – and the fact that it sounds as though Ismay was running around like 'a headless chicken' – the Fifth Officer's reaction seems not unreasonable.

So was there confusion about what procedures to be followed? Was Ismay aware of the crew's inexperience in these matters?

Having already established that Ismay was the only executive officer of the White Star Line on board the *Titanic*'s maiden voyage, Senator Smith asked him if he had occasion to consult with Captain Smith about the progress of the ship. After first denying this, Ismay then agreed that he and the Captain had discussed the time of the ship's arrival in New York as being scheduled for 5am on Wednesday morning, April 17th. Ismay assured Senator Smith that this was considered perfectly achievable and that there was nothing to be gained by arriving in New York ahead of schedule.

'Watertight' Smith

There were obviously a great number of people who could be brought before the Senate Inquiry, which was convened in the Waldorf-Astoria hotel in New York and subsequently at the Senate in Washington. Senator Smith was a flamboyant figure, accused by the British press at the time of using the inquiry as a grandstand for his own larger-than-life personality. They dubbed him '*Watertight Smith*'. This was due to the remark he made when he asked Great Uncle Bertie whether a watertight compartment was somewhere passengers could safely shelter from the ravages of the sea.

Lightoller's opinion

This greatly annoyed Lightoller, for he mentions in his autobiography:

> With all the good will in the world, the 'Enquiry' could be called nothing but a complete farce, wherein all the tradition and customs of the sea were continuously and persistently flouted. Such a contrast to the dignity and decorum of the Court held by Lord Mersey in London, where the guiding spirit was a sailor in essence, and who insisted, when

necessary, that any cross-questioner should at any rate be familiar with at least the rudiments of the sea. One didn't need to explain that 'going down by the bow' and 'going down by the head' were one and the same thing. Nor, that watertight compartments dividing the ship were not necessarily places of refuge in which passengers could safely ensconce themselves, whilst the ship went to the bottom of the Atlantic, to be rescued later, as convenient... neither was it necessary to waste precious time on lengthy explanations as to how and why a sailor was not an officer, though an officer was a sailor.

Then we come to Great Uncle Bertie's own admission of, as it were, 'bending the truth' – a passage so crucial that it surely bears the most careful scrutiny.

In Washington it was of little consequence, but in London it was very necessary to keep one's hand on the whitewash brush. Sharp questions that needed careful answers, if one was to avoid a pitfall, carefully and subtly dug, leading to a pinning down of blame on someone's luckless shoulders... a washing of dirty linen would help no one.

The inference here seems to be that my great uncle considered the senators in the American inquiry to be a load of idiots, while those with some maritime experience asking the questions in London were smart men; and a sharp lookout had to be kept in order to avoid being trapped into an admission that the loss of the *Titanic* was a fiasco implicating the White Star Line, including J. Bruce Ismay and thus J. Pierpont Morgan, in an act of gross negligence. This could have been the end of the company, and so led to Great Uncle Bertie and the surviving members of *Titanic*'s crew finding themselves out of a job. And, after thirteen years with the White Star Line, Great Uncle Bertie had established a very comfortable lifestyle. His house not only had ten bedrooms but included stabling, a bakery and a tennis court. In fact, there is a possibility that Second Officer Lightoller was privy to a deception that far eclipsed the crime of pure negligence. Despite his later admissions of circumventing the truth at the inquiries, it is possible that the real story behind the *Titanic*'s sinking has never been properly revealed.

I suspect it is likely that, in later years, this evasive action of Lightoller's at the inquiries weighed heavily upon him, for he admitted to a number of further contentious issues in confidence to both his sister and his wife before he died.

Chapter 10
Unexpected revelations

Senator Smith loses patience

Senator Smith began to lose patience with Lightoller during what amounted to a cross-examination of a man who appeared unable to give a straight question a straight answer. During my great uncle's time on the witness stand, the fact is that Senator Smith and Lightoller took against each other. The senator later toured the *Titanic*'s sister ship, the *Olympic*, where he would have learned at first hand exactly what a 'watertight compartment' was. However, that knowledge would have been gained too late to serve in his battle of words with my recalcitrant great uncle.

George Harder's testimony

Great Uncle Bertie's scathing remarks in his autobiography regarding Senator's Smith's lack of maritime knowledge, especially regarding watertight compartments, now seem somewhat churlish in the light of an account relating to the ineffectiveness of some of the *Titanic*'s watertight compartments. This was in the testimony of a survivor, George Harder, who also gave a deeply concerning report of his experience in what my great uncle would have considered to be a fully tested lifeboat. Harder's first-hand account shows quite clearly that Lightoller's contention that the lifeboats were effectively tested during the ship's trials on Belfast Lough was flawed. The Second Officer had the gall to tell the first day of the inquiry that, during the so-called 'sea trials', which of course were not even at sea, only six lifeboats were actually lowered all the way to the water. Even then he did not say how many men, if any, were actually in these boats during their testing. What he did say to the senators, however, is that he did not consider that the davits – the lifeboat lowering equipment – would actually support the boats when they were loaded with their full complement of people.

The ineffectiveness of the crew in both the lowering of the lifeboats and in their general handling is graphically illustrated in this testimony of George Harder, the twenty-six-year-old from Brooklyn, who described himself to the committee as a manufacturer, and who was accompanied on the voyage by his wife, Dorothy. Having stated his age, address and occupation to the committee, Harder was asked by Senator Smith where his First Class cabin was situated.

'We had E50 on E deck.'

'What occurred Sunday night between eleven and twelve o'clock?' asked the senator. Harder replied:

> About a quarter to eleven, I went down to my stateroom with Mrs Harder and retired for the night, and at twenty minutes to twelve we were not asleep yet, and I heard this thump. It was not a loud thump; just a dull thump. Then I could feel the boat quiver and could feel a sort of rumbling, scraping noise along the side of the boat. When I went to the porthole I saw this iceberg go by. The porthole was closed. The iceberg was, I should say, about fifty to one hundred feet away. I should say it was about as high as the top deck of the boat. I just got a glimpse of it, and it is hard to tell how high it was.

'What did you do then?' the senator asked.

> I thought we would go up on deck to see what had happened; what damage had been done. So we dressed fully and went up on deck, and there we saw quite a number of people talking; and nobody seemed to think anything serious had happened.

There were such remarks as, 'Oh, it will only be a few hours before we will be on the way again.' I walked around the deck two or three times, when I noticed that the boat was listing quite a good deal on the starboard side; so Mrs Harder and myself thought we would go inside and see if there was any news. We went in there and talked to a few people, and all of them seemed of the opinion that it was nothing serious. A little while after that an officer appeared at the foot of the stairs, and he announced that everybody should go to their staterooms and put on their lifebelts.

Senator Smith was keen, at this point, to establish the time frame of Harder's recollections of events. 'How long was that after the collision?'

That, I think, was a little after twelve o'clock; that is, roughly. So, we immediately went down to our stateroom and took our lifebelts and coats and started up the stairs and went to the top deck. There we saw the crew manning the lifeboats; getting them ready; swinging them out. So we waited around there, and we were finally told, 'Go over this way; go over this way.' So we went over toward the first lifeboat.

That boat was filled, and so they told us to move on to the next one. I have been told that Mr Ismay took hold of my wife's arm – I do not know him, but I have been told that he did – and pushed her right in. Then I followed.

'How far did you have to step from the side of the ship into the lifeboat?' asked Smith.

I should say it was about a foot and a half. Anyway, you had to jump. When I jumped in there, one foot went in between the oars, and I got in there and could not move until somebody pulled me over.

Now comes one of the most damning parts of Harder's testimony: a statement that was never mentioned in any reports of the disaster and which, if properly investigated, might well have resulted in a charge of criminal negligence being brought against the White Star Line and its owners.

Failure to close the watertight doors

George Harder continued his testimony:

> I forgot to say that when I went down into my stateroom in order to get the lifebelts, when I came out of the stateroom with the lifebelts I noticed about four or five men on this E deck, and one of them had one of those T-handled wrenches, used to turn some kind of a nut or bolt, and two or three of the other men had wrenches with them – Stilson wrenches, or something like that. I did not take any particular notice, but I did notice this one man trying to turn this thing in the floor. There was a brass plate or something there.

Senator Smith quickly interjected: 'Was it marked WT?'

> Yes; it was marked WT, and I do not know whether it was a D after that or something else. A few days before that, however, I noticed that brass plate, and, naturally, seeing the initials WT, I thought it meant watertight doors, or compartments.

The senator was anxious to be precise: 'Was it in the floor?'

> Yes. On E deck. It was on the starboard side of the boat, in the alleyway. I think this brass plate was situated between the stairs and the elevators. The stairs were right in front of the elevators, and right in between there, I think, was this brass plate.
>
> I heard one of these men with the wrenches say: 'Well, it's no use. This one won't work. Let's try another one.' They did not seem to be nervous at all; so I thought at the time there was no danger; that they were just doing that for the sake of precaution.

Senator Smith strained to get the facts absolutely correct. 'Did any of those men state, in your hearing, the importance of being able to turn that bolt or not?'

Harder replied that they did not, so Smith continued: 'Did you gather from what you saw that it was connected directly with the watertight compartments?'

Yes, sir, I thought it was. I related the incident to Mr Bishop after the accident.

Dickinson Bishop and his wife had become friends with Harder and Dorothy during the voyage and ended up in the same lifeboat at the sinking. Bishop was called before the hearing as a witness on its eleventh day and confirmed that Harder had told him about his suspicions of the watertight doors not being closed.

Senator Smith persevered with his questioning: 'How large was this plate?'

The plate was, I should say, about ten inches or a foot wide. It was about circular. I do not remember anything else about it, except that it had the initials WTC or WTD or something like that.

Later in his testimony, Harder addressed Senator Smith again on the matter of the watertight doors, or compartments:

There is just one other point I might mention, Senator. I have been told that all these watertight doors operate by electricity from the bridge – all the doors below the decks, in the hold – and that this one deck, F, below E deck, had doors that were worked by hand, and that this plate in the floor of E deck, to which I have referred, was the place where they were to be turned by hand.

On the question of the lifeboats, Harder commented:

We got into the lifeboat, which was either number 5 or number 7.

'Who was in charge of it?' asked Senator Smith.

Mr Pitman. That was the second boat to leave on the starboard side, as far as I could see. As we were being lowered, they lowered one side quicker than the other, but we finally reached the water safely, after a few scares. When we got down into the water, somebody said the plug was not in; so they fished around to see if that was in, and I guess it was in. Then, they could not get the boat detached from the tackle, so they fussed around there for a while, and finally they asked if anybody had a knife, and nobody seemed to have a knife. Finally, one of the passengers had a knife in his possession, and they cut some rope.

Lifeboat chaos

This surely confirms beyond any reasonable doubt that the lowering of lifeboats on the stricken liner was a chaotic procedure. So once again this disproves Great Uncle Bertie's assurance to the Senate Inquiry that he had fully and successfully tested the lowering of the lifeboats during the ship's sea trials. For this reason, Senator Smith at the Senate Inquiry was anxious to be clear about the procedure carried out in the lowering of the boats:

'Do you wish to be understood as saying that the tackle or gear by which this boat was lowered did not work properly?'

Harder replied:

That was on account of the crew up on the deck. They had two or three men on each side, letting out the rope, and they let out the rope on one side faster than the other. That caused the boat to assume this position going down (*indicating*) and we thought for a time that we were all going to be dumped out. We finally reached the water all right. Then the next job was to get the ropes at each end of the boat, the bow and the stern of the lifeboat, detached. I understand there was some new patented lever on there, some device that you pull, and that would let loose the whole thing. Whether they did not know that it was there or not, I do not know; I presume they did not, because they did not seem to get it to work, and they finally had to resort to this knife.

We started to pull away from the ship. We had, as I learned afterwards, about forty-two people in the boat.

Senator Smith then read from a statement already made to the committee by Third Officer Pitman who was in charge of the lifeboat: 'He says that they rowed off some distance from the side of the ship. Is that correct? And that there were cries for help, and the passengers in that boat would not permit him, Mr Pitman, to go to their relief.'

We were afraid of the suction. The passengers said, 'Let us row out a little farther.' So they rowed out farther, perhaps about a half a mile. There we waited around a while. This other boat came alongside, either boat number 7 or boat number 5. We tied alongside of that, and they had twenty-nine people in their boat, and we counted the number of people in our boat; and at that time we only counted, I think it was, thirty-six. So we gave them four or five of our people in order to make it even, as we were kind of crowded.

Senator Smith was naturally surprised at this remark: 'This was a large lifeboat that you were in?'

Yes, sir, it was the regular size lifeboat. They say those boats hold sixty people, but we had only the number of people I have mentioned; and, believe me, we did not have room to spare. Then we waited out there until the ship went down. After it went down, we heard a lot of these cries and yells. You could not distinguish any sounds.

Then we stayed around there until daybreak, when we saw the *Carpathia* and we rowed the distance; I do not know how far it was; probably two miles; it might have been less.

Icebergs everywhere!

Senator Smith then asked: 'You agree with the others that in the morning the presence of these icebergs in large numbers was disclosed? How large, in your judgment, was the largest one?'

Yes; I counted about ten of them around. I should not like to
make a statement in regard to [their size] Senator, because I
am very poor at distances and dimensions. They were of good
size.

So from George Harder we learn that certain of the watertight
doors to the watertight compartments of the *Titanic* were
probably never closed properly after the ship struck, possibly
hurrying the sinking by more rapid filling of the hull with
water than the captain and designers of the ship would have
expected. We also learn that Lightoller's self-congratulatory
remarks about the testing and suitability of the lifeboats were
probably inaccurate, making the ship's Second Officer
potentially liable to an accusation of gross negligence. Like
Joseph Bruce Ismay, the owners of the *Titanic* and her officers,
both those who survived and those who perished, Lightoller
received no reprimand.

However, the lifeboat issue was only one of my great
uncle's dubious pronouncements at the official inquiries that
followed the sinking. His sister (my grandmother) and his
widow (my great aunt) both implied to me in their own way
that, throughout the remainder of his long and illustrious
career, ghosts from that fatal night and his duplicitous
behaviour afterwards continued to haunt him.

Chapter 11
Cross-examination

Ismay on the spot

On day eleven of the US Senate Inquiry, Joseph Bruce Ismay was grilled, not by the flamboyant Senator Smith, but by Senator Jonathan Bourne, a Republican senator from Oregon. He was at pains to clarify the actual ownership of the White Star Line and Ismay's part in this, as the corporate owners were in fact American. Although the *Titanic* was a British-built and British-registered vessel, the ultimate owner was J. Pierpont Morgan, the American billionaire.

Establishing ownership of the *Titanic* and the White Star flag under which it sailed was of great importance for, had the real owner of the vessel been proven to have committed any kind of criminal negligence, or worse still contrived a deliberate sinking, one of the world's most powerful men would have been in deep trouble. Apart from any insurance claim being negated, there would have been huge claims for compensation lodged by survivors and relatives of those lost in the disaster.

Amazingly enough, neither White Star nor its ultimate owners, the International Mercantile Marine Company, were ever prosecuted for any form of negligence in the construction, handling or fatal collision of the *Titanic*; nor did International Mercantile Marine or any of its interlinked subsidiaries ever pay out a penny in any form of compensation.

The whole thing seems rather reminiscent of British banks sinking the nation's economy and instead of being penalised, getting away with it scot-free and what is more, being given billions of the public's money to bail them out!

Great Uncle Bertie, being the most senior surviving officer, was the first of the crew to be questioned on that first day of the Senate Inquiry.

The Second Officer v Senator Smith

Asked by Senator Smith what position he had held during his time with the White Star Line, Lightoller replied, 'Fourth, Third, Second and First Officer.' He told the inquiry that he'd been with the White Star Line for thirteen years and three months, working his way up to the rank of First Officer.

Yet he had been demoted from First to Second Officer on the *Titanic*, in favour of William Murdoch, shortly before the ship's maiden voyage. One of the unanswered questions raised at the start of Lightoller's testimony was why, having arrived at the rank of First Officer with the company, he had been demoted after the *Titanic*'s trial runs in Belfast Lough and replaced at the request of Captain Smith by William Murdoch. This sudden change was brought about by Smith's seemingly impulsive desire to bring Henry Wilde on board as Chief Officer. This meant that Murdoch and Lightoller both had to take a step down in rank, the demoted Lightoller replacing David Blair as Second Officer. Blair was then asked to sit out the voyage so that the rest of the ship's complement could remain unchanged.

Lightoller makes little reference to his demotion, but it couldn't have been easy for him to lose the coveted position of First Officer. Captain Smith's avowed reason for making the change was that Murdoch had served as First Officer in the *Titanic*'s sister ship, *Olympic*. Yet the *Olympic* was almost as doomed a vessel as the *Titanic*, having been badly damaged in a collision with a Royal Naval cruiser. In two more disastrous episodes the ship hit a sunken wreck and later lost a propeller blade, almost running aground in the process. How strange to pick such a disaster-prone officer to replace Lightoller. Interestingly enough, it appears that Captain Smith and Murdoch were in some way related; so perhaps, after all, it was just a case of nepotism at sea!

The damage sustained by the *Olympic* cost the White Star Line dear and gave rise to one of the most extraordinary maritime conspiracy theories, which I later found myself investigating.

Of course, it is so easy with hindsight to say, 'If only...'; but the rearrangement of the pecking order in the *Titanic*'s ranks might just possibly have been a contributory factor to the disaster. If, for instance, Lightoller had remained as First Officer of the ship, then he would have most likely been on duty on the bridge that fatal night when the iceberg was first sighted. Would he have reacted differently from Murdoch? Would he have issued different or swifter orders?

Unanswered questions

Other questions must remain for ever unanswered. If those on the bridge and in the crow's nest had been in possession of binoculars, might the iceberg have been sighted sooner? When the original Second Officer, David Blair, was excluded from the voyage, he disappeared with the key to the locker in which the binoculars were kept. Without easy access to this, Lightoller offered to purchase some more when they reached New York.

Subsequently, at the Board of Trade Inquiry in London, Sir Ernest Shackleton, the distinguished polar explorer, stated that although some seamen preferred to rely on the naked eye, others found binoculars helpful in distinguishing distant objects. Knowing their possible usefulness at sea it seems strange that Lightoller did not seek permission to force open the locker containing the binoculars or at least discuss the problem with his Captain well before the start of the transatlantic voyage. It was just one more in a lengthy catalogue of oversights, omissions and carelessness which cost the lives of 1,535 innocent people.

As a matter of interest, I recently discovered that Blair's set of keys for the binoculars locker was auctioned in April 2010, fetching sixty thousand pounds in the sale rooms of Henry Aldridge and Son in Wiltshire!

The sea trials

We now come to Senator Smith's next set of questions to Lightoller, which related to the 'so-called sea trials' of the *Titanic* – the senator's words, not mine. From this phrase it is plain that the senator considered that the sea trials were inadequate for the recently launched liner, by far the biggest ever built. Lightoller described the trials as taking place exclusively in Belfast Lough, a stretch of water only open to the sea at one end and a mere fifteen miles in length. It appears that *Titanic* was never subjected to proper trials in the open sea over a longer distance. Even if *Titanic* was sailing on these trials at a mere fifteen knots, well below her potential top speed, this was less than an hour's trip to one end of the lough and back again. Lightoller confirms that the trials consisted mainly of turning circles but not at the ship's full speed. It is now widely believed that *Titanic* was close to her full speed of approximately twenty-two knots when an iceberg was only fifty yards ahead. Sir Ernest Shackleton's testimony given at the London inquiry stated categorically that, based on his vast experience of sailing in polar seas, he would advise eleven knots maximum in these circumstances for something as big as *Titanic*.

Senator Smith then asked Lightoller how long the so-called sea trials had lasted, to which my great uncle replied that it was approximately five hours. However, he said he was unable to judge from his station at the stern of the ship as to whether or not full engine power was used. When asked if there had been straight-line sailing tests he replied that *Titanic* had steamed up the lough and back again, taking two hours each way. If the lough was only fifteen miles long by Lightoller's estimate, then the ship could only have been travelling very slowly at about 6.5 knots.

Great Uncle Bertie was well into his seventies when I last saw him and he was as bright as a button. As someone who had spent his life sailing the seas of the world for about sixty years, both under sail and power, he would have had to rely on mathematical calculations to plot his course on numerous occasions. There is no way that he could have thought that the *Titanic* cruised fifteen miles in two hours at her full speed, when he has already said that her acknowledged top speed was in the region of approximately 21.5 knots.

Unhelpful Lightoller

From the very first day of the US inquiry, Second Officer Lightoller appeared confused and on several occasions downright obtuse in giving testimony. So, was he still in a state of shock from the sinking? Or had secret meetings with Ismay on board the rescue ship, *Carpathia*, persuaded him to frame his story in a particular fashion?

Senator Smith asked Lightoller if there was anyone from the White Star Line on board the ship during the sea trials, to which his reply was: 'None was seen.'

'Was Mr Ismay on board?' asked the senator.

'Not to my knowledge, sir.'

The senator sought further clarification: 'Did you hear afterwards that he was on board?'

'No sir,' replied Lightoller and further affirmed that there was no one on board for the sea trials who represented the British Government.

Senator Smith then turned to the matter of life-saving equipment. 2,225 people embarked on the *Titanic*'s maiden voyage and there were definitely not enough lifeboats for all of them. However, at the time of the sinking there was an 1894 law in force requiring only a minimum of sixteen lifeboats to be carried by ships over ten thousand tons. The *Titanic* weighed in at 46,328 tons, but as the 1894 law was still in force, White Star was not compelled to carry sufficient boats for more than about a third of its passengers. In fact the ship ended up carrying lifeboats for slightly less than half of those aboard. Prior to the loss of the *Titanic*, authorities had believed that on the busy Atlantic shipping routes there would always be other vessels at hand should a ship get into difficulties. Unfortunately, no one had taken into account the possibility of a giant liner crashing into an iceberg in the middle of the night and sinking before help could reach her.

Lightoller and lifeboats

Senator Smith asked Lightoller if the *Titanic*'s life-saving equipment was complete. When my great uncle answered in the affirmative, the senator continued: 'Of what did this consist?'

'The necessary number of lifeboats,' was the imprecise answer.

The senator was beginning to get exasperated by Lightoller's inconclusive answers.

'I wish you would say how that is determined.'

'By the number of people on board,' was the scant reply.

'You do not know how many there are on board until you are ready to start?'

'Yes, there must be life-saving apparatus for everyone on board, regardless of accommodation.'

The senator then asked: 'How many lifeboats were there?'

'Sixteen.'

Senator Smith seemed to think that he had received a proper answer at last – except that the final specifications of the *Titanic* at sea quite clearly state that twenty lifeboats were on board. How could Great Uncle Bertie get it that wrong? Certainly four of the lifeboats were of a collapsible type, one of which the Second Officer ended up clinging to. Nevertheless, there were twenty lifeboats just the same. But then of course Lightoller could only have lowered sixteen in the *Titanic*'s sea trials, as the collapsible ones were for last-minute emergency evacuation and presumably not via the davits.

Nevertheless, this anomaly regarding the number of lifeboats available on the doomed ship appears to have gone unnoticed by Smith, as he proceeded to the subject of the testing of lifeboats prior to the maiden voyage: 'Was a test of the lifeboats made before you sailed for Southampton from Belfast?'

Lightoller replied that all the gear was tested. He went on, under cross-examination, to state that in these tests, and at his orders, all the boats were lowered. He was then asked to describe this exercise in detail and replied: 'All the boats on the ship were swung out and those that I required were lowered down as far as I wanted them – some all the way down and some dropped in the water.'

Only six lifeboats tested

Lightoller then admitted that only six out of the twenty lifeboats on the ship were actually fully tested by being lowered all the way into the water, yet he had just told the senator that all the lifesaving equipment was fully tested! It would surely not have been beyond the bounds of possibility for one or more of the untested lifeboats to have had faulty running gear, leading to a disastrous hitch in getting survivors away from a sinking ship?

In point of fact, according to survivors, this is exactly what happened. Yet another example of Lightoller's muddled and misleading answers. Was this a 'cover up' for his inefficiency, or merely the slovenly safety procedures observed within the White Star Line?

There are conflicting reports about the amount of time it took during the *Titanic*'s sinking to launch all the lifeboats and apparently, as clearly shown in both *A Night to Remember* and James Cameron's *Titanic*, there is a very real likelihood that some of the lifeboats had problems on being lowered from the

Lux Vestra: Let Your Light Shine
The Lightoller coat of arms, hand-painted by the author's grandmother –
Charles Herbert Lightoller's sister, Gertrude

TOP The author's grandmother, Gertrude Lightoller
BOTTOM LEFT An early portrait of Great Uncle Bertie in uniform
BOTTOM RIGHT The author's mother, Elizabeth Hannah

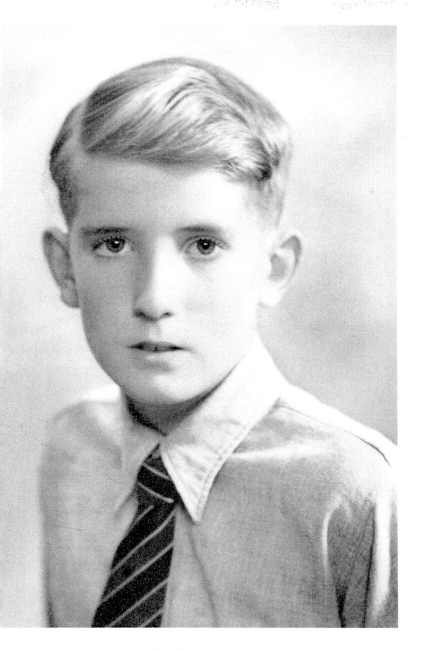

The author aged twelve

TOP LEFT An advertising poster for *Olympic* and *Titanic*: 'The largest steamers in the world'
TOP RIGHT Just before departing, Fourth Officer Boxhall (centre) prepares to close the
gangway door for the last time (Lightoller is believed to be the officer on the right)
BOTTOM Second Officer Lightoller on the bridge of the *Titanic*

Two Witnesses in Titanic Hearing Before Committee at Capitol

TOP *Titanic*'s surviving officers: (seated) Third Officer Herbert John Pitman,
(standing, left to right) Fifth Officer Harold Godfrey Lowe,
Second Officer Charles Herbert Lightoller, Fourth Officer Joseph Groves Boxhall
BOTTOM LEFT Pitman and Lightoller awaiting the American inquiry
BOTTOM RIGHT A newspaper sketch from the inquiry

TOP Captain Arthur Henry Rostron of the *Carpathia* being presented with a trophy by
Mrs J. J. ('Molly') Brown, for his services in the rescue of *Titanic*'s survivors
BOTTOM LEFT Joseph Bruce Ismay, White Star Line's Chairman and Managing Director
BOTTOM RIGHT The *Olympic* showing damage sustained in the collision with HMS *Hawke*

TOP The damage to *Olympic* close up
BOTTOM *Olympic* and *Titanic* – could they have been switched?

Charles Herbert Lightoller in Royal Navy uniform

ship. Noting that the majority of the lifeboats were only lowered halfway during their testing, Senator Smith remarked:

'Of course, part of the way down would not do anybody much good on a sinking ship!'

To which Lightoller replied: 'It is principally the gear we test. The lifeboats we know to be all right.'

It is interesting to note that Lightoller later commented that many of the lifeboats did not have lights, extra oars or biscuits. So in fact, apart from an inadequate and random system of lowering the lifeboats, each individual lifeboat had not been properly checked. As most of the lifeboats were stored on the top deck, Lightoller, when asked, judged the drop to the water to be about seventy feet – a very long way to lower a boat with a pulley system that may never have been fully tested with the ship afloat. As already mentioned, many of the passengers and crew were too busy with 'morning worship' to ensure their earthly safety by an official lifeboat drill.

Chapter 12
Dodging the question

No recommendations

Lightoller was recalled to the US inquiry on its fifth day and on this occasion Senator Bourne asked if he would have any recommendations to make, following his experience of the tragedy. Surprisingly it seems that Lightoller had nothing to say on this subject. It would have been quite obvious to even someone with limited seagoing experience that the entire sinking was caused by a series of disastrous mistakes on the part of the White Star Line itself and by the ship's designers, as well as the Captain and certain officers. Throughout the inquiries in New York and later in Washington and London, it became increasingly obvious that, when in doubt, Lightoller replied that he had no expert opinion to deliver and so chose to remain silent.

Searchlights

Even the advisability of having searchlights on board received the comment from Lightoller that, while they might be useful to those behind the light, it might temporarily blind those on the other side of it: a remark that would surely be treated as 'glimpses of the obvious'. Senator Bourne persisted:

'Would it not be worthwhile to carry searchlights on transatlantic liners, just for the sake of picking up in certain localities? Would it not be useful in detecting ice on a dark night?'

Lightoller replied that he could not say without experiencing it; another case of doing a body-swerve around a crucial question. Lightoller also had no comment to make on the possible advantage of having binoculars for officers on the bridge and the lookouts in the crow's nest. He specifically avoids mention of the key to the binoculars' locker being kept by David Blair who did not sail on the maiden voyage.

Lookouts

Senator Smith then asked Lightoller about the men in the crow's nest. Apparently they were paid an extra allowance for this duty. Lightoller said he always selected men that he knew and had worked with in the past, men who were highly experienced at this very special job: in particular, a man named Symonds, who had been with Lightoller for a number of years on the *Oceanic*. However, Symonds later testified that he was not in the crow's nest at the time of the fatal collision with the iceberg!

Lightoller also stated that even if the crew in the crow's nest were skilled at their job, he would never rely on them. This might seem strange to a non-mariner, as the crow's nest – being situated high up on a ship's forward mast – must surely have a better sight of approaching objects than the view from the command bridge far below. Although this may at first seem to be a strange remark by Lightoller, Sir Ernest Shackleton's later testimony in London clarifies the point Great Uncle Bertie was attempting to make.

In fact, two men – Fleet and Lee –were in the crow's nest at the time of the collision. At some point Lightoller remarked that when there were two men in the crow's nest there was always the risk that they might engage in conversation and so allow their attention to wander from the job in hand – namely, keeping a sharp lookout forward of the ship's line of progress.

Lightoller talks with Ismay

Earlier in the day at the inquiry my great uncle gave a long and rambling account of a discussion with Bruce Ismay during the voyage. He commented that it merely concerned another ship of the Line called the *Cedric*, on which Lightoller wanted to travel back to Britain from New York. Apparently sailors are booked on a voyage-by-voyage basis and *Cedric*, shortly due to leave New York for Britain, would get Lightoller and other of his fellow officers home quicker and also keep the crew together. He persuaded Ismay to send a telegram to the *Cedric* asking her to await the arrival of the *Titanic* in New York: something that, via a return telegram, *Cedric* refused to do.

Lightoller continued with what seemed a complete *non sequitur* by launching into a conversation he had with Ismay on board the *Carpathia* after the sinking:

> I may say that at the time Mr Ismay did not seem to be in a good mental condition to finally decide anything. I tried my utmost to rouse him for he was obsessed with the idea and kept repeating that he ought to have gone down with the ship because he found women had gone down.

The strange case of Luis Klein

We now come to a section of the US inquiry which, were it not concerning such a serious matter, would surely rival the best of the routines in a Marx Brothers movie. My great uncle was recalled yet again on the ninth day, when Senator Smith began by asking him:

'Mr Lightoller, are you familiar with the ship's crew of the *Titanic*, when she left Southampton, and at the time of the accident?'

Another rather insolent answer: 'You are speaking of the seamen, are you, sir?'

'Yes,' said Senator Smith.

'Yes, sir,' answered Lightoller.

We then get into what almost amounted to a comedy double-act as Senator Smith continued:

'Have you ever known Luis Klein?'

'Not amongst the seamen.'

'Was there such a member of the crew of the *Titanic*?'

'I am given to understand that there was one man named Klein who was a Second Class barber. That man is personally known to me.'

'Did he survive?'

'He did not.'

'Who was the barber? Do you recall him by name?'

'Klein.'

'No; I do not mean him. This was the assistant – Klein, the man you speak of. I want to know who the barber was. Who was the principal barber on that ship?'

'The First Class barber?'

'Yes.'

'I forget his name, sir.'

'Do you know whether he survived?'

'He did not.'

'I would like to have you be very sure of that, sir.'

'Of which, sir?'

'Of that last statement. Will you kindly make yourself very certain of that? I am in communication with the First Class barber, who is an American, the only American, I believe, who was in the crew, and I would like to have you think over whether there was more than the one First Class barber, so that we have no conflict about this man.'

'To the best of my knowledge and belief the First Class barber was not saved, unless I have been misinformed.' At this point Lightoller apparently consulted his notes before correcting himself. 'I am very sorry, sir; I see that the First Class barber is here.'

'What is his name?'

'Whitman – or Whiteman?'

Senator Smith than carefully spelt out the name, as he made a note of it.

'W-h-i-t-m-a-n?'

'Yes.'

'I have just been handed by a surviving passenger a memorandum, and he says that this barber is now in New Jersey. Would you like to correct your statement in that respect?'

'Yes; I would. The First Class barber evidently is the survivor.'

'But you are positive that the only Klein in the crew did not survive?'

'He did not survive.'

'Did you see a man here in my office this week who claimed to be Luis Klein, a surviving member of the crew of the *Titanic*?'

'I believe that I did, sir.'

Senator Smith, now definitely playing the part of a courtroom prosecutor: 'Had you ever seen him before?'

'Never.'

The stowaway

Senator Fletcher then interrupted the proceedings by asking Lightoller: 'Could he have been the stowaway who was found in one of the lifeboats?'

'I really could not say, sir. I know the man that Senator Smith speaks of as being in his office, and I certainly never saw him before.'

'You recall that the stowaway, referred to as having sneaked into the boat with a shawl and a dress on, had a broken arm? This man you saw in my office did not have a broken arm, did he?'

'Not as far as I could see, sir.'

'Do you know who made up the list of the surviving members of the crew?'

'I made up the list for the seamen and Hardy, the assistant Second Class steward, made up a list for the victualling department.'

'Was any list made on the *Carpathia* regarding the survivors of the crew?'

'Yes.'

Senator Smith then asked: 'And you feel that you have an accurate list?'

'I feel that I have. I went through all the seamen and firemen personally.'

This exchange on the ninth day of the US investigation gives some insight into the labyrinthine complexities facing the senators, as they strove to unravel the mysteries of the *Titanic*'s sinking. It also shows how, during the investigations, Great Uncle Bertie was, in some of his recollections of events, both confused and seemingly contradictory.

The press and the mysterious Mr Klein

It would seem apparent from the line of Senator Smith's questioning that he was privy to a number of stories in the American press relating to the mysterious Mr Klein. Had my great uncle also read some of these papers he might have answered Senator's Smith's questions about Klein somewhat differently.

For instance, a *Washington Press* report on April 21st stated:

The long arm of the senate of US, backed by the department of justice, reached out today to Cleveland Ohio and carried the subpoena to Washington of Luis Klein, a Hungarian and member of the crew of the ill-fated *Titanic*, who has made important statements concerning the recent disaster to the White Star Line.

Senator Smith said that Klein had made statements to the city editor of a newspaper in Cleveland, that he had made like statements to the Hungarian consul and that he had been closely examined and had remained unshaken. United States attorney Denman at Cleveland wired to Senator Smith that he had served the subpoena.

Klein sounds the alarm

So, what was this all about? A report of Klein's supposed statement to the press read:

> There was a ball following a banquet of some kind going on down below when I went up on watch at 9.30 o'clock. And the captain and the officers were there with many passengers. After the party, the stewards sent the champagne and wines that were left over to the crew. I know that many of them were drunk. A passenger standing at the rail saw something dead ahead or maybe a little to the starboard. 'Look quick! See the hill over there?' I saw it was a big iceberg and ran for the bridge. The Third Officer was coming and yelled to me to ask what was the matter? I couldn't stop to answer. I was too excited. I ran for the spar with the crow's nest on it and shouted to the lookout I knew was up there to give the alarm. Not a word did I hear, so I started up the spar. It was less than a minute after I left the promenade deck that I got to the top of the spar and found the lookout fast asleep. I rang the alarm bell myself.

The disappearance of Mr Klein

Apparently Klein, who spoke no English, was thoroughly cross-examined by Hugo Varga, the Austro-Hungarian Vice Consul, who stated that the man steadfastly stuck to his story. However, if Klein spoke no English, how did the press come by this detailed and dramatic story? And how could there be only one man in the crow's nest when Lightoller had made clear that there were two? Was there even the remotest possibility of truth in Klein's statement? If there was, then this would cast a devastating shadow of criminal negligence across the entire episode of the sinking. However, despite the subpoena, the mysterious Klein never appeared at the Senate Inquiry and in fact was never seen again. What happened to Klein? Did he really exist? Was he a member of the *Titanic*'s crew? Did my great uncle actually know him? Why did he disappear? He certainly would not be the first vital witness called before an American official inquiry to disappear! It seems to be just one more mystery in a series of mysteries surrounding the *Titanic* disaster.

The *Gazette Times* in Pittsburgh on the morning of April 22nd 1912 carried the shocking headline:

'Titanic sailors drunk' says one of them.

Beneath this there was a subheading:

Man in crow's nest sound asleep when ship strikes iceberg.

Chapter 13
Confused evidence

More questions

On the ninth day of the US inquiry, Senator Smith continued to question Lightoller: 'You said that there was no suction in the sea at the time and place where the *Titanic* disappeared.'

'Exactly,' replied Lightoller, 'the suction was hardly noticeable.'

'When you said that you twice found yourself against the grating of the blower when in the water, were you pushed back to it by suction of any kind?'

Lightoller replied that the force of the water racing through the blower carried him back against it.

Senator Smith then changed the direction of his enquiry. 'When you last saw the *Titanic* did you see numerous people on deck?'

'Do you mean before I left?' In fact, here he seemed to be admitting 'leaving' the ship, whereas he later stated categorically that 'the ship left me'.

'Before you left the side of the *Titanic* and while you were in the water?'

'You could not see the decks from that point.'

'You could not see the upper decks?'

'I mean that I could not see anyone on her decks.'

The senator seemed unable to grasp Great Uncle Bertie's point which is that, if he was in the water, he would be some fifty to seventy feet below the main decks of the ship and therefore unlikely to have a clear sight of any people there. However, the truculent Second Officer was not prepared to explain this to a man he obviously considered to be an ignorant landlubber.

Later Lightoller described climbing on board an upturned lifeboat along with a number of other survivors. At daybreak they were taken aboard lifeboat number 14 and he recalls that, as there was no officer on board, he automatically took charge. Asked if, as it was now light, he had cruised around the scene of the wreck, he replied that he did not as he saw no wreckage or floating bodies of any sort.

This remark of his is strange in the light of various descriptions from other sources that there were numerous bodies with life jackets on in the water.

The British inquiry

Great Uncle Bertie was obviously delighted to get back to Great Aunt Sylvia and the children, although his appearance before the London Board of Trade Inquiry into the sinking forced him, of his own admission in his autobiography, to take part in something of a 'whitewash'.

On the eleventh day of this London enquiry, my great uncle faced cross-examination by the Solicitor General. In particular, he was asked about a telegraphic message handed to him by the Captain of the *Titanic* while on the bridge in the afternoon of April 14th; that is to say, just a few hours before the collision with an iceberg.

Lightoller agreed with the Solicitor General that he relieved First Officer Murdoch on the bridge at around 1pm. He was then asked: 'Do you remember Captain Smith showing you something during this time?'

'Yes.'

'Just tell us what it was.'

'Captain Smith came on the bridge during the time I was relieving Mr Murdoch. In his hand he had a message, a

Marconigram. He came across the bridge and, holding it in his hands, told me to read it. The actual wording of the message I do not remember.'

'Did you see that it was about ice?'

'It had a reference to ice.'

'Do you remember between what meridians?'

'Yes, I particularly made a mental note of the meridian – 49 to 51 degrees.'

'That would be 49 to 51 west?'

'Exactly.'

The Solicitor General then consulted a copy of the message in question and quoted the latitude of ice being described as at 42 degrees north. He then asked Lightoller: 'Do you recollect that 42 north indicated to you that this was where you were likely to go?'

'I would, had I taken particular notice of the latitudes, though as a matter of fact, latitude with regard to ice conveys so very little.'

'Is that because ice tends to settle north to south?' asked the Solicitor General.

To which Lightoller replied: 'We take very little notice of the latitude because it conveys very little.'

'Then do you attach more importance to the longitude?'

For once, Lightoller gave a positive reply: 'Far more.'

'I notice that your recollection of the message is that you recollect 49 and 51 degrees west.'

'That is the longitude.'

'Did you form any sort of impression at the time as to what time of the day or night you were likely to reach the area indicated?'

To which Lightoller said: 'Not of the time.'

However, Lightoller then suggested that he later detailed off one of the junior officers to work out when they would reach the ice. He explained that he went off watch ready to return on duty at six in the evening, convinced that the ship would not reach the area where icebergs had been reported before he returned to the bridge at 6pm.

He was then asked if, on returning to the bridge at six, he noted the speed of the ship from the number of revolutions of the engines – shown as 75. He estimated a speed of 21.5 knots, about 24 miles an hour, which was approaching the liner's top speed. However, this, as far as Lightoller was concerned, was a speed never achieved during the ship's so called 'sea trials' in Belfast Lough.

Which Marconigram?

Lightoller said he called Sixth Officer Moody to calculate the time they were likely to reach the ice field, based on the Marconigram Captain Smith had shown him earlier. The Solicitor General then continued with his questioning:

'Had the Marconigram about ice with the meridians on it been put up on any kind of notice board?'

'Most probably on the notice board in the chart room.'

'So when you gave Mr Moody those directions, he had the material to work with?'

To which Lightoller responds: 'Exactly.'

'And he calculated and told you about eleven o'clock you would be near the ice.'

'Yes.'

'That is to say an hour after your watch finished?'

'Yes. As a matter of fact I have come to the conclusion that Mr Moody did not take the same Marconigram that Captain Smith had shown me. I came to the conclusion that we should be at the ice before eleven o'clock, by the Marconigram I saw.'

'In your opinion, when in point of fact would you have reached the vicinity of the ice?'

'I roughly figured out about half past nine.'

'Then Mr Moody made a mistake?'

'He probably had not noticed the 49 degree wireless (Marconigram). There may have been others. He may have made his calculations from one of the others.'

'When he came on your watch and said that you would get to the ice at about eleven, did you say anything about it to him?'

'No.'

'It was important to you?'

'As far as I remember and I thought I would not bother him just at that time.'

Full speed in an ice field!

Thus it seems that forty-two thousand tons of ship was ploughing through the North Atlantic at something approaching full speed in the pitch dark and was in fact due to enter the dangerous ice fields some considerable time earlier than calculated. Great Uncle Bertie suspected this – but did nothing about it – he simply returned to his cabin!

My great uncle was recalled again on day twelve of the British inquiry. During this there was much complicated cross-examination regarding the preparation and lowering of the lifeboats. Lightoller appeared to have lost precious time by ordering women and children down to the promenade deck, only to discover that the windows there were sealed shut – resulting in a further order for them all to proceed back up to the boat deck. The British Solicitor General asked Lightoller if any orders were given regarding getting into the boats.

Women and children first!

'The Captain gave it to me.'

'What was the order?'

'I asked the Chief Officer if we should put women and children in the boats and he said "No". I found the Commander (Captain Smith) and asked him if we should put the women and children in and he said: "Yes, put the women and children in and lower away." That was the last order I received from the ship.'

An interesting question now followed from the Solicitor General to Lightoller:

'In your judgment is it possible to fill these lifeboats when they are hanging as full as you might fill them when they are waterborne?'

'Most certainly not.'

Lightoller then explained that a lifeboat lowered with the full complement of passengers would probably not survive the slow and laborious lowering some fifty feet down the side of the ship. In fact, it was seventy feet from boat deck to water. Thus, he reasoned, a lifeboat would never, in practical terms, contain the numbers it was designed for, quite apart from the fact that, even if they were all full, about half of the passengers would still be left behind!

Missing messages

Telegrams, or Marconigrams as the wireless communications between ships at the time were called, reared their ugly head again on day fourteen of the British inquiry. Sir Robert Finley again addressed my great uncle:

'You have heard that a message was sent, according to the evidence, to the *Titanic* which read: "For transmission to Cape Race from the *Amerika*"?'

'Yes.'

'What was the course of business with regard to messages communicated by the Marconi operators to the Captain or officers?'

'It is customary for the message to be sent direct to the bridge. If addressed to Captain Smith or the captain, it is delivered to Captain Smith personally if he was in his quarters or on the bridge. If he is not immediately get-at-able, it is delivered to the senior officer on the watch. Captain Smith's instructions were to open all telegrams and act on your own discretion.'

'And you are positive that you never heard anything of either of these telegrams?'

'Absolutely positive.'

'What were you doing in the afternoon about two o'clock, which is when the telegram from the *Amerika* was likely to have reached the *Titanic*?'

'I was below.'

'When did you come up?'

'At six o'clock.'

'And from six you were on the bridge?'

'From six till ten, with the exception of half an hour for dinner.'

'You were on the bridge?'

'I was.'

'And nothing was said by anyone about such telegrams?'

'There were no telegrams received by me, nor did I hear of any telegrams.'

'A message such as that would be of great importance?'

'I have no doubt it would have been immensely important to me if it referred to ice.'

As the hearing progressed it appeared that not one, but two messages were received by the wireless operators of the *Titanic* regarding warnings of ice, and these came from two separate ships. Yet it seems that the *Titanic* just kept ploughing on through the ocean at something approaching her top speed.

Referring to a vital piece of paper with the word 'ice' written on it, with latitude and longitude marked underneath, Lightoller is at pains to explain that, because it lay on the chart room table and was not written on the proper form, he ignored it!

Chapter 14
Important witnesses

Members of the Board

The British Board of Trade Inquiry was officially entitled the British Wreck Commissioner's Inquiry, because there were on the board several men with considerable nautical experience. These included Professor J. Harvard Biles, who held the Chair in naval architecture at Glasgow University, and Rear Admiral S. A. Gough-Calthorpe, Royal Navy retired. Also present on the board were Edward C. Chaston, Senior Engineer Assessor, Captain A. W. Clarke from Trinity House and Commander F. C. A. Lyon, Royal Navy retired.

The American inquiry into the disaster was carried out by no less than seven worthy US senators, none of whom appeared to know much, if anything at all, about the sea and its inherent dangers. Nor did they seem able to fully appreciate the way in which common sense and professional procedures had knowingly or unknowingly been flouted by the owners and officials of the doomed *Titanic*.

Great Uncle Bertie, in his autobiography *Titanic and Other Ships*, is extremely scathing of the senators' 'landlubbery' approach, compared to what he considered to be the more professional and knowledgeable conduct of the British inquiry. However, the US inquiry, which started in New York before moving to Washington, had to be staged with all due haste after the sinking, no doubt to satisfy pressure from all sides demanding an immediate and diligent search for the truth of an event that had taken so many wealthy and respected Americans to a watery grave.

Enter Sir Ernest Shackleton

Despite the presence of several nautical experts on the board of the British inquiry, when it came to the crucial matter of ice it was thought expedient to call someone with a more profound first-hand knowledge and experience of the subject – the renowned polar explorer, Sir Ernest Shackleton.

Born in February 1874, just one month before Charles Herbert Lightoller, Shackleton had a short but action-packed life, dying in January 1922, some thirty years before my great uncle. Ernest Shackleton, an adventurer of Anglo-Irish descent, was hailed as the great British hero of antarctic exploration; although, in his first experience of the polar regions, as Third Officer on Captain Scott's *Discovery* expedition of 1901, he had to be sent home early on health grounds. Like Joseph Conrad's *Lord Jim*, and perhaps Great Uncle Bertie, the rest of Shackleton's life was a catalogue of heroic deeds aimed at mitigating an earlier perceived personal failure. In January 1909, Shackleton and three companions made a record 114-mile march south, by far the closest anyone at the time had got to the South Pole. For this he was knighted by King George V.

Shackleton confirmed to the inquiry that, on a clear night, an iceberg would be visible at about five miles. If the *Titanic* was steaming at some twenty miles per hour or more and an iceberg was visible at five miles then there would, in theory, have been ample time for even a ship as large as *Titanic* to take avoiding action and change course within the fifteen minutes between sighting the iceberg and reaching it, even if her speed were not reduced.

Dark icebergs

Shackleton was then asked about so-called 'dark' icebergs, ones with a core of rock and soil that have eroded and broken away from an arctic shore. He replied that he had occasionally seen icebergs of varying colours. The question was then put to him that, if on a clear night a normal iceberg was visible at about five miles, at what distance would a dark iceberg be visible? To which he replied that it might be as little as three miles. Although this would make it necessary for an emergency change of course, it might still be possible to avoid a collision. However, there is no evidence to suggest that the iceberg that sank the *Titanic* was in fact a 'dark' iceberg. It is well documented that, on scraping the side of the iceberg, the *Titanic*'s deck was littered with pieces of pure ice both large and small. There were no reports of rock or soil being found in these deposits.

Shackleton then explained that, in a dead calm sea, which apparently was the case on the fateful night, there may have been very little sign of telltale breakers visible at the base of the giant iceberg. 'If you first see the breaking sea,' he said, 'then you look for the rest and you generally see it.' Crucially he explained, 'That is in the waterline. I do not say very high, because from a height it is not so easily seen.'

He concluded: 'If you are on the sea-level it may loom up.'

Sighting an iceberg

The Attorney General was quick to grasp this point:

'Your view would be that you could detect bergs of that kind better from the stem than you could at the crow's nest? Do you think it is of advantage in clear weather to have a man stationed right ahead at the stem as well as in the crow's nest?'

'Undoubtedly,' replied Shackleton, 'if you are in the danger zone – the ice zone.' He also pointed out that he would slow right down in any ship when there was a chance of encountering ice.

'Supposing you were going at 21 or 22 knots?' asked the Attorney General.

Shackleton was adamant. 'You have no right to go at that speed in an ice zone, where it has been reported. I think that the possibility of an accident is greatly enhanced by the speed the ship goes.'

Again, he reiterated the need for a man at the bow of the ship, even on a fine, clear night. Shackleton also made a comment about those posted in the crow's nest; a man on his own is less likely to be distracted than if he had a companion with him.

He told the inquiry that on his trip to the South Pole he was in a vessel very much smaller than the *Titanic* and proceeded in ice zones at no more than five to six knots. On the subject of binoculars and their use at sea, Shackleton commented that, although some seamen prefer to use the naked eye to scan the sea ahead, 'you have the whole range of the horizon in one moment with your eyes but you localise it by using glasses' (by which he meant binoculars).

When it was pointed out to Shackleton that at three o'clock in the afternoon of April 14th there was no wind and the temperature fell abnormally for the time of year, he replied that he would consider that in this case he was approaching an area that might have ice in it. He suggested that all liners in the Atlantic should slow to ten knots as soon as they know there is any possibility whatsoever of coming across icebergs, particularly at night-time.

He further contended that in recent years speed had become of the essence in Atlantic crossings of passenger vessels. Top speeds had increased and owners of these lines had been known to press their officers and crew to get their passengers to their destination with all due haste. This might be particularly so in a case where the owners of the ship were on board.

The lifeboat disaster

Returning to the subject of lifeboats, upon which the survival of those at sea depends, the inquiry questioned Captain Rostron of the *Carpathia*, the rescue ship of the *Titanic*'s survivors. The Captain provided the following details of his own ship's safety equipment. The *Carpathia* was 13,600 tons, carried about three hundred crew and 750 passengers. Small as this was by comparison to the *Titanic*, she carried eighteen lifeboats capable in theory of carrying 1,224 people. On this particular voyage the total crew and passengers on board were a little over a thousand, providing more than adequate provision for safety – unlike the arrangements on the *Titanic*, where an original provision had been made for sixteen sets of davits capable of lowering away thirty-two lifeboats. These would have had a capacity of four thousand people, more than the maximum carrying design of 3,600 passengers and crew.

However, on the basis of the existing Board of Trade's regulations at the time, White Star decided to carry only twenty lifeboats with a maximum capacity of 1,178. Although designed for thirty-two lifeboats, Ismay insisted on only twenty to avoid cluttering the decks so that First Class passengers could enjoy greater space to 'promenade'. Only after the *Titanic* disaster did the Board of Trade revise its regulations, making it mandatory for all ships to carry sufficient lifeboats for everyone aboard and, most importantly, to carry out regular lifeboat drills.

The Master of the *Carpathia*

The Master of the *Carpathia* described to the US inquiry in some detail the distress signals he received from the stricken *Titanic*:

> I was just in bed and the first Marconi operator came to my cabin and came right up to me and woke me and told me he had just received an urgent distress signal from the *Titanic*, that she required immediate assistance, that she had struck ice

and giving me her position. I immediately ordered the ship to be turned around.

Captain Rostron explained that the position given by the *Titanic* in her message placed her at 41.46 north, 50.14 west – about fifty-eight miles from the *Carpathia*'s position as she turned around. Asked at what speed his ship could travel, the Captain replied that ordinarily it would be 14 knots but that night he pushed it to over 17 knots and steamed as fast as they could, having received the *Titanic*'s distress signal at 10.35pm. *Carpathia* was judged to be still some twenty miles from the *Titanic* by 2.40am. At that distance they were able to see a green flare in the sky, the White Star's night signal.

Rostron remarked that he assumed the *Titanic* was still afloat at that point. He told the inquiry that, en route to assist the stricken *Titanic*, his ship was constantly changing course to avoid icebergs. Unlike the *Titanic*'s captain, Rostron had situated two men at the stem, right in the bows of his ship to look out, as well as one man in the crow's nest. He said that at night, irrespective of ice warnings, he always stationed at least one lookout in the bows of the ship and one in the crow's nest. He further explained that it is usual for lookouts to spot an iceberg when it is two or three miles away and that to only have a sighting of it when it is as near as a quarter of a mile is most uncommon.

Chapter 15
Ismay's part in the drama

Ismay and Lightoller

So was Ismay Great Uncle Bertie's nemesis? He was certainly the man to whom my great uncle was accountable throughout his entire career with the White Star Line.

Charles Herbert Lightoller was born in Chorley, Lancashire, a mere twenty miles or so from Crosby, where Joseph Bruce Ismay had entered this life some twelve years previously. There the tenuous connection ends. Ismay was educated at Harrow, one of England's most prestigious and most expensive schools. Lightoller's schooling was scant and, running off to sea at thirteen, his studies were mainly confined to literally 'learning the ropes' aboard some of the world's most demanding sailing ships. Rightly, his education could be said to have been obtained at the University of Life. Ismay came from a shipping family. His mother, Margaret Bruce, was the daughter of a ship owner, Luke Bruce. Her husband, Thomas Ismay, was the senior partner in the shipping company Ismay, Imrie and Co and was also the founder of the White Star Line.

J. Bruce Ismay's education was completed in France, before he was apprenticed to his father's firm. Following this, he toured the world, prior to moving to New York to work for the White Star Line. There, at the age of twenty-six, he married Julia Delaplaine, with whom he had five children. Just three years after his marriage, Ismay moved his family back to Britain when he became a partner in his father's firm. When Thomas Ismay died in 1899, he left the family business to his son. Three years later Ismay agreed to merge the firm with an American shipping conglomerate, the International Mercantile Marine Company. However, by 1904 Ismay had become head of International Mercantile Marine with the backing of the all-powerful billionaire J. P. Morgan.

Lightoller's life prior to setting sail on board the *Titanic* could hardly have been more different from that of his ultimate commander, J. Bruce Ismay. In his autobiography *Titanic and Other Ships* Lightoller says: 'Few boys that go to sea are born to be drowned.' Grandma Gertrude told me on more than one occasion that Great Uncle Bertie would boast to her that the sea would never drown him.

Giants of the sea

In the early years of the twentieth century, Cunard, White Star Line's chief competition on the transatlantic run, launched her two magnificent liners, the *Lusitania* and *Mauretania*. Ismay was determined to beat Cunard at their own game and decided to build a trio of ships that would be bigger, faster and more luxurious than those of any of his rivals. He aimed, with his vast leviathans, to dominate once and for all the sea between Britain and America.

He firmly believed that this plan would generate considerable revenue for his company in two ways. First, it would offer wealthy First Class passengers unparalleled luxury in their surroundings on a transatlantic voyage; they would pay handsomely for the privilege of being transported effortlessly across a vast ocean in such comfort. But also, provision would be made – on the decks below the millionaires, aristocrats and affluent middle-class passengers – for an unprecedented number of those travelling Third Class or 'steerage'.

The cost of a *Titanic* ticket

It is interesting to note the price discrepancy between the cost of the best First Class Parlour Suite at £870 and a steerage ticket at £3, which meant that the richest of the rich were paying almost three hundred times as much for the same journey as many Irish who were leaving their own country to settle in America. At a comparable rate today, that would mean roughly $106,000 for a First Class Parlour Suite on the *Titanic* and $362 to travel steerage.

The giant trio of oceanic liners that Ismay was obsessed with launching on a vast and capricious ocean were the *Olympic*, the *Titanic* and the *Britannic*; *Titanic* was the second of these superliners to be built by the Belfast shipping yard, Harland and Wolff. To accommodate the ship's luxurious features, including a vast promenade for the wealthy to stroll along, Ismay decided to reduce the number of lifeboats in davits, as opposed to the four collapsibles, from forty-eight to sixteen, the minimum required under the then-current Board of Trade regulations. As the dream ship prepared to sink for ever beneath the ocean that Ismay had expected to conquer, he escaped in a lifeboat reserved for women and children, an act he would be haunted by for the rest of his life.

Ismay accused

At the Senate inquiry, some passengers testified that during the voyage they had heard Ismay pressurising Captain Smith to go faster with the object of arriving in New York ahead of schedule and so generating some useful press coverage. One passenger also claimed to have seen Ismay flaunting one of the iceberg warning messages at the dinner table before placing it back in his pocket. It was suggested by another that Ismay had asked for a speed test to take place on April 14th not long before the collision. However, this has never been proved although, as Sir Ernest Shackleton's testimony to the British inquiry made clear, the *Titanic* appeared to have been travelling far too fast on the fateful night.

The crucial telegram

On the afternoon of Sunday April 14th at approximately five o'clock, Mrs Emily Ryerson and Mrs Marian Thayer were watching the sun go down from the First Class Deck of the *Titanic*. Sadly, both of them were to lose their husbands when the ship sank some nine hours later. They were approached by J. Bruce Ismay, dressed as usual in his best, who enquired if their staterooms were comfortable. Emily Ryerson had some slight acquaintance with Ismay through mutual friends on board and he thrust a Marconigram at her, announcing that they were now among icebergs. When a remark was made about the speed of the ship, he replied that although the ship had not been going fast, they were to start up extra boilers that afternoon. Noticing that the message also mentioned a distressed liner, the *Deutschland*, which appeared to be in difficulties, Mrs Ryerson later remarked that Ismay scoffed at the idea of the *Titanic* coming to its rescue, announcing that 'they had no time for such matters as our ship wanted to do the best'. Something was also said about getting in on Tuesday night. When questioned later about this conversation Ismay, whom many people considered to have a remarkable memory, could only recall the presence of Mrs Thayer.

Ismay in love

Frances Wilson, in her book *How to Survive the Titanic, or the Sinking of J. Bruce Ismay*, shows Marian Thayer to be a vivacious woman who was able to spellbind all those with whom she came in contact. She was a collector of 'life stories' – people talked to Marian Thayer as they would to no one else, and Ismay found her particular kind of American openness totally fascinating. There was no doubt that his interest in her was something that would stay with him for much of his life. Whenever he saw her, he looked for a reason to detain her; and on the afternoon of April 14th on the deck of the *Titanic* he had the perfect excuse. Although it was to Emily Ryerson that he showed the Marconigram, it was Marian Thayer to whom his attention was drawn, before placing the message from the *Baltic* back in his pocket.

Frances Wilson tells us that: 'While Mrs Ryerson told the story to the press Mrs Thayer said nothing about the encounter herself. When the time came for Mrs Ryerson to sign her affidavit, it may have been Marian Thayer who persuaded her to withhold Ismay's comments about lighting further boilers to get through the ice, remarking "the poor man was going through enough already."'

The relationship between Ismay and Marian Thayer continued by letter long after the sinking and it is said that he read and reread her letters every night.

My second cousin, Lady Louise Patten, in her book *Good as Gold* maintains that it was on Ismay's orders that *Titanic* continued sailing at speed after the impact with the iceberg when, had the ship remained stationary, she might have taken less water and therefore stayed afloat until help arrived. This and other interesting claims by Lady Patten were verified during conversations with both her mother and her grandmother, Sylvia Lightoller, my great aunt.

Part Three
Stories and Conspiracies

Chapter 16
Death and Divine Power

Into the spotlight

Yes, life had been tough for both our hero and his nemesis, but in radically different ways. These two men probably understood each other well, but knew how to respect their different places in the scheme of things: Ismay the rich, reserved head of a successful international shipping firm, and Lightoller, a regular ship's officer. However, a terrible event changed everything, putting them on an equal footing, as Great Uncle Bertie became the confidant and co-conspirator of the head of the company for which he worked. Although he was only the Second Officer on the doomed *Titanic*, the luxury liner's sudden demise pitched Lightoller into the position of being the only person in the entire world that Ismay could turn to for support in the immediate aftermath of the sinking of the White Star Line's prize possession.

As in many apparently unexpected disasters, chaos reigned immediately prior to the death of the *Titanic*. Over the past hundred years, the shortcomings of both captain and crew immediately after the fatal collision have been well documented. There have been some hundred and fifty books published about the sinking, from Lawrence Beesley's *The Loss of the SS Titanic* in 1912, to Frances Wilson's 2011 book which tells the compelling story of my great uncle's boss in *How to Survive the Titanic, or the Sinking of J. Bruce Ismay*. This last book paints possibly the clearest picture yet of what made Ismay the man he was and what ultimately destroyed him.

After a lifetime of adventure, there is no doubt that Great Uncle Bertie had been inescapably caught up in a web of unfolding historical events which, for the past hundred years, have captured the interest and emotions of millions around the world.

So, what kind of man was Charles Herbert Lightoller? To me as a child, he was rugged, sometimes cantankerous and full of tales of the sea, many of which he may have created especially for my benefit.

The plot thickens

Although I only spent a comparatively short space of time with the Reverend William Hannah, his intellect, enthusiasm and wit remain clear in my memory. For all of my childhood a large framed photograph of Canon Hannah, as he later became, was displayed on the top of my mother's beloved piano, a Collard and Collard from Belfast (according to the flowery inscription on the lid).

Charles Herbert Lightoller's life read like one of the boys' adventure books I used to read, filling my head with wild tales and brave deeds. If Great Uncle Bertie's life was one of adventure, then Joseph Bruce Ismay's was one of romance – although not the kind of romance attached to affairs of smouldering passion but more of a tall, athletic young man inhibited in personal relationships but keen to use his huge wealth and power to impress high society on both sides of the Atlantic. Someone who inherited a fleet of ships and sold them to an American multibillionaire, Ismay liked to look his best at all times, keen to stamp his taste and style on everything he touched. Thomas Ismay was a hard act for his son Bruce to follow. Ismay Senior created thousands of jobs in the Belfast shipyard and harnessed the power of steam to drive his gigantic liners across the Atlantic. He put his entire fleet at Queen Victoria's disposal to transport men, weapons and ammunition to far-off South Africa to bolster up the British army's fight against the Boers. However, there is no doubt that Charles Herbert Lightoller was fashioned in the likeness of a hero and, long after the *Titanic* episode, that is how many remembered him.

Two old ladies at a funeral

As I sat there at my Great Uncle Bertie's funeral, wedged between the two old ladies, they looked much of an age to me, a mere thirteen-year-old. In fact, they just looked very old. When you're a child, eager to become an adult, anyone over forty is old and once someone reaches sixty, they are ancient. On that cold, depressing December day in 1952 Grandma Gertrude looked no older at eighty-four than her sister-in-law, Great Aunt Sylvia, at a mere sixty-seven. Gertrude had already outlived her brother Bertie and, like my mother, her daughter Elizabeth, was destined to live an extremely long and healthy life. But then, of course, Great Uncle Bertie had lived a particularly hard life: not just his arduous adventures in great sailing ships and his fruitless search for gold in the frozen wilds of the Yukon, but in the secrets of the *Titanic*'s sinking and his relationship with J. Bruce Ismay, that he now took with him to his grave.

John Calvin's dictate, so abhorred by Mary Baker Eddy, was a simple one: if you're good, you go to Heaven; and if you're bad, you go to Hell. This creed was positively medieval in its simplicity. So I wonder where my great uncle thought he was headed to as he shuffled off this mortal coil.

Goodbye Bertie, goodbye Bruce

What a life my Great Uncle Bertie had! Bereft of a mother and then of a father, with a succession of tough and seasoned sailors as his only surrogate parents and the sea as his unforgiving mistress. What really happened during the most defining moments of his life, when, at the age of thirty-three and not yet halfway through his life, the huge bulk of the

Titanic began to sink beneath the surface of the icy North Atlantic? According to the testimony he gave to the *Christian Science Monitor*, it was his firm belief in God's life-preserving hand that plucked him from a watery grave. It is certainly a dramatic and life-affirming piece.

I have no clear recollection of what happened after the crematorium doors had finally closed behind my great uncle's coffin. I suppose Great Aunt Sylvia was waiting around for her husband's ashes to be delivered in an urn. My mother later told me that they had been scattered over the crematorium's Garden of Remembrance, which I found rather strange. Surely it would have been more fitting for them to have been consigned to the flowing waters of the Thames beside the Richmond boatyard that Charles Herbert and Sylvia had run for many years together? I seem to remember that there were not that many people present in the Mortlake Chapel or at the small reception back at the boatyard afterwards. It was certainly in steep contrast to the departure from this life of the disgraced and guilt-ridden man who had, in all probability, persuaded the hero Lightoller to perjure himself.

Joseph Bruce Ismay's funeral service in 1937, fifteen years prior to my great uncle's, was held at St Paul's church in Knightsbridge, with close to a hundred and fifty mourners present. These included several top-ranking army officers, at least one earl and one lord, plus others of the great and good including the director of what was by then the Cunard White Star Line and a representative of Harland and Wolff, builders of the *Titanic* and her sister ship the *Olympic*.

Why were all those people there? Was it to pay their last respects to a great man? Or was it to give thanks for the burial of troublesome memories – the memories of a fateful night some twenty-five years previously when J. Bruce Ismay may or may not have sunk the *Titanic*? During those intervening years, Ismay had already buried himself, metaphorically, by taking premature retirement and moving to a home in a remote part of Ireland. From there he involved himself in a number of charitable foundations for *Titanic* survivors and others deprived of life or livelihood by the sea. He was seventy-five when he died; when Great Uncle Bertie's ashes were scattered in the Garden of Remembrance in Mortlake, he had lived for seventy-eight years. Had he not continually had a foul-smelling pipe clamped between his teeth, he would no doubt have lived a good deal longer, for he was assuredly a lion-hearted man.

A Christian Scientist's view

Lightoller's fellow Christian Scientist Lawrence Beesley's description of the sinking of the *Titanic* gives a first-hand account of the momentous drama, the telling of which still enthrals the world today. My great uncle's account of the sinking, both in his autobiography and before the inquiries in New York and London, appears manifestly inaccurate and complex by comparison.

Beesley's comments from *The Loss of the SS Titanic* were certainly a cry for far greater accountability in the safety of those at sea. As his book was published within months of the tragedy, this account adds the kind of first-hand immediacy of on-the-spot reporting.

Think of the shame of it, that a mass of ice, of no use to anyone or anything should have the power fatally to injure the beautiful *Titanic*, that an inscrutable block should be able to threaten, even in the smallest degree, the lives of many good men and women who think and plan and hope and love – and not only to threaten, but to end their lives. It is unbearable! Are we never to educate ourselves, to foresee such dangers and prevent them before they happen? All the evidence of history shows that laws working unknown and unsuspected are being discovered day by day: as this knowledge accumulates for the use of man, is it not certain that the ability to see and destroy and the threat of danger will become one of the privileges the whole world will utilise? May that day come soon. Until it does, no precaution too rigorous can be taken, no safety appliance, however costly, must be omitted from a ship's equipment.

Quite early on at the beginning of the voyage, Beesley notes that 'an almost clock-like regularity of two vibratory movements was what attracted my attention; it was while watching the ship roll, that I first became aware of the list to port.' He notes, with regard to the night of the collision: 'I am sure we were going faster that night at the time we struck the iceberg than we had done before.'

Beesley goes on:

Now I am aware that this is an important point and bears strongly on the question of responsibility for the effects of the collision. The impression of increased vibration is fixed in my memory, so strongly that it seems important to record it. Two things led me to this conclusion – first, that as I sat on the sofa, undressing, with bare feet on the floor, the jar of the vibration coming up from the engines below was very noticeable and second, that as I sat up on the berth reading, the sprung mattress supporting me was vibrating more rapidly than usual: this cradle-like motion was always noticeable as one lay in bed, but that night there was certainly a marked increase in the motion.

To verify this, Beesley refers to a plan of the ship.

It would be seen that the vibration must have come almost directly from below... the saloon was immediately above the engine room and my cabin was next to the saloon.

Beesley continues:

There came what seemed to me nothing more than an extra heave of the engines and more than usually obvious dancing motion of the mattress on which I sat... any list to port would have tended to fling me on the floor. And yet, the explanation is simple enough: the *Titanic* struck the berg with a force of impact of over nine million foot-tons: her plates were less than an inch thick and they must have been cut through as a knife cuts through paper.

Once on deck, the passengers assembled there became acutely aware of some impending catastrophe. The roar and hiss of steam escaping from the ship's boilers was so loud that conversation was virtually impossible.

Beesley reports that by about 12.20am the crew were working on the lifeboats from the top deck, which was the boat deck. He was standing there on the starboard side. An officer appeared from the First Class deck and shouted loudly above the noise of the escaping steam: 'All women and children get down to the deck below and all men step back from the boats.'

Lightoller gets it wrong

It seems likely that the officer in question was my great uncle. And, as other testimonies verify, both he and Captain Smith got the lifeboat procedures quite wrong, forgetting that, unlike her sister ship *Olympic*, *Titanic*'s saloon deck had been glassed in.

The confusion amongst both passengers and crew, when it came to the loading and lowering away of the ship's lifeboats, was vividly captured in James Cameron's movie *Titanic*. There had certainly been no lifeboat drill since the ship set forth from Southampton, and Lightoller's rehearsal of the boats during the ship's leisurely sea-trial cruise up and down the Belfast Lough obviously left much to be desired.

Beesley then describes a ship, which is sometimes referred to as the 'mystery' ship. Realising *Titanic* was sinking, Captain Smith hailed this vessel by means of both rockets and Morse code signals. Smith placed this 'mystery' ship at only about five miles from his own vessel, which was in deep distress. Lightoller certainly saw the rockets go up to signal distress, while Seaman Hopkins in Boat 13 affirmed that he saw the lights of the unknown ship and, together with the survivors in his lifeboat, rowed towards it. However, slowly but surely, the 'mystery' ship's lights moved away, until they disappeared completely into the night.

Divine Power

According to Beesley, as the lifeboats were lowered from the sinking ship, Lightoller ordered newly married men out of the boats where they were seated with their recently wed wives. His orders were, 'Women and children first!' – an order he might not have so scrupulously obeyed had he known that the rescue ships he believed would surely reach them were in fact further away from the scene than he imagined.

Beesley, like Great Uncle Bertie, was a Christian Scientist and a devout follower of Mary Baker Eddy's teachings. His philosophising on page 88 of his book *The Loss of the SS Titanic*, good though his reportage is, seems somewhat unclear in attitude, bearing in mind the teachings he subscribed to. This particular passage is prompted by Beesley witnessing the rescue from the icy water of one of the *Titanic*'s stokers, too drunk to comprehend anything that was going on around him. As a result, the benefit of his presence in the lifeboat was discussed by several survivors, unsure whether a more suitable person could have been picked from the ocean.

> These discussions turned sometimes to the old enquiry: 'What's the purpose of it all? Why the disaster? Why this man saved and that man lost? Who has arranged that my husband should live a few short happy years in the world, and the happiest days in those years with me, these last few weeks – and then be taken from me?' I heard no one attribute all this to a Divine Power, who ordains and arranges the lives of men and as part of a definite scheme send such calamity and misery in order to purify, to teach, to spiritualise. I do not say there were not people who thought and said they saw Divine Wisdom in it all – so inscrutable that we in our ignorance saw it not; but I did not hear it expressed, and this book is intended to be no more than a partial chronicle of the many different experiences and convictions.

So Beesley and Lightoller were both convinced, through their belief in Christian Science, that there must be such a thing as Divine Providence. And yet the way that Beesley talks about it here and the way Lightoller describes it in the *Christian Science Monitor* do not, on the face of it, seem that far removed from the Calvinistic creed so abhorrent to the founder of Christian Science, Mary Baker Eddy. Calvin's belief was that the Good find everlasting salvation in the wonders of Eternal Heaven, while the Bad suffer torment for ever in the depths of Hell. All very medieval by the sound of it, but did this mean that Great Uncle Bertie always regarded himself as Good with a capital G? Did he justify as 'good' his lies and general subterfuge in front of the official inquiries into the sinking? How did he feel about inadequate and improperly tested lifeboats, manned in an emergency by crew not properly trained in life-saving procedures? Did he know that this most valuable prize of the White Star Line was not as well prepared for every eventuality as she should have been; and did he know full well that the *Titanic* was travelling too fast into an ice field without properly placed lookouts in the bows, vital binoculars and helpful searchlights?

Chapter 17
Omissions

Avoidance

Although my great uncle's autobiography is entitled *Titanic* in large letters on its cover, with the subtitle *and Other Ships* in very small letters underneath, out of the book's 344 pages only thirty are actually taken up with the catastrophic sinking of the 'unsinkable' ship. The remaining 314 pages are packed with Lightoller's adventures aboard 'other ships'. I wonder why he dwelt so briefly on what must have been the most dramatic event in the long catalogue of dramas in his life at sea.

Riches indeed

In 1907 the White Star Line opened a new route to New York, based on Southampton, as it was somewhat closer to London and therefore considered more convenient for the high class passengers the line was seeking.

From Second Officer on the *Oceanic*, Lightoller moved up to First Officer on the *Majestic*. Sailing from Southampton meant a move for him and his family from Crosby in Lancashire to Netley Abbey, a village on Southampton Water. The Lightollers' new home certainly demonstrated the status and salary that accompanied the position of a senior officer on a major transatlantic shipping run. It was the kind of home only afforded today by a successful City of London banker on a five-million-pound yearly bonus.

Not the ideal Captain

White Star's managing director J. Bruce Ismay was not by any manner of means a contented man at this time. The Cunard Line had snatched his *Oceanic*'s crown as 'Queen of the Seas' with their larger and faster ships, the *Lusitania* and the *Mauretania*. The thirty-one-thousand-ton *Lusitania* now held the coveted 'Blue Riband' for the fastest Atlantic crossing. However, Ismay was his father's son and like Thomas before him he had one eye on power and glory and the other firmly fixed on profit. Being the fastest across the Atlantic meant burning up a great deal of coal, and coal cost money.

In 1909 the White Star Line launched the first of its great seagoing behemoths, *Olympic*. Following her first run to New York in 1911, she quickly became the ship of choice for the wealthy and famous when visiting the US. She was captained by Edward J. Smith, whose record of commanding White Star liners was anything but perfect. Quite apart from the disastrous incident with HMS *Hawke*, which almost wrote off the *Olympic*, Smith had managed on previous occasions to run the *Republic* aground in New York's harbour and later do exactly the same thing in Rio de Janeiro with the *Coptic*!

Yet Ismay would later praise the man he had chosen to command the White Star Line's most treasured possession, the *Titanic*, on its way to a watery grave. He declared: 'Captain Smith is a man with a very clear record. I should think very few commanders crossing the Atlantic have as good a record as Captain Smith had, until he had the unfortunate incident with the *Hawke*.'

Ismay said that he considered that the collision with the Hawke had not shaken his confidence in this man and he had no reason to doubt that Captain Smith had 'quite got over the mishap'.

Some five years before *Titanic*'s sinking, Smith had described his career at sea as 'uneventful', stressing that: 'In all my experience, I have never been in an accident... of any sort worth speaking about.'

Obviously, running a couple of ships aground was not worth speaking about; and as for never having been in an accident, unfortunately he was about to be a principal player in the most famous maritime accident of all.

The dream ship

Not even the *Olympic* could compete with Ismay's dream ship – the *Titanic*. This floating hotel offered the absolute best of everything for the true high-net-worth individual, including two millionaire suites at a staggering $4,350 for a one-way ticket. You certainly needed to be a millionaire, or more likely a multimillionaire, to afford these prices for a sea trip.

Ismay was a shrewd businessman who saw the advantage of offering those who could afford it luxury travel that set them apart from other mere mortals. They would pay ridiculous sums for the privilege accorded them by travel on a White Star monster. However, Ismay was determined to wring as much profit from his luxury lines as possible, and so provision was made on these ships for the many emigrants deserting Europe for a hoped-for 'new life' in America. These Third Class or 'steerage' passengers' accommodation, although an improvement on the horrors of earlier transatlantic passages for the poor, were a million miles from the truly opulent cabins and staterooms of the rich and famous travelling in the White Star Line's new ships.

One of Captain Edward Smith's tragically optimistic and oft-quoted remarks when referring to the *Titanic* was: 'I cannot imagine any condition that would cause a ship to flounder. Modern shipbuilding has gone beyond that.'

At what point he had to admit that this was a wild inaccuracy has long been open to debate. Was it only when he realised that the ship beneath him, the so-called 'unsinkable', was about to take its final plunge to a watery grave? Or, as some believe, was it in fact some considerable time before this?

What went wrong?

Unlike Captain Smith, Chief Officer Wilde and First Officer Murdoch, my great uncle had not served on the *Titanic*'s sister ship *Olympic*. These officers do not appear to have been involved in the new ship's sea trials on Belfast Lough, after which Lightoller had a mere two weeks to familiarise himself further with the *Titanic* before her maiden voyage. No one has so far clearly identified why White Star officials decided, almost at the last moment before the *Titanic*'s maiden voyage, to bring in Wilde as Chief Officer. What it certainly did mean was that the three men most responsible for the new giant liner had previously sailed in and were particularly familiar with her sister ship *Olympic*, a ship that had been badly damaged in the collision just months before with HMS *Hawke*.

Great Uncle Bertie comments on the unexpected 'reshuffle' of officers in his autobiography *Titanic and Other Ships*:

> Unfortunately, whilst in Southampton we had a reshuffle amongst the senior officers. Owing to *Olympic* being laid up, the ruling lights of the White Star Line thought it would be a good plan to send the Chief Officer of *Olympic*, just for one voyage, as Chief Officer of *Titanic*. This doubtful policy threw both Murdoch and me out of our stride; and, apart from the disappointment of having to step back in our rank, caused quite a little confusion.

One wonders whether this demotion resulted in any drop in Lightoller's salary. He certainly makes no mention of this.

Quite apart from any other confusion, we know that the redundant Third Officer Blair left the *Titanic* quite forgetting he had the keys on him to the vitally important locker where the binoculars were kept. Many more careless mistakes of this nature were to dog the first and last trip of the giant liner.

Ice warnings

Lightoller declares in his autobiography that the *Titanic* was not making her full speed on the night of the catastrophe –

although Sir Ernest Shackleton made it quite clear to the British inquiry following the sinking that *Titanic*'s speed was far too fast for that of any ship travelling at night through ice-fields. However, Great Uncle Bertie writes about what he calls 'circumstances that never occurred before and can never occur again'. He states:

> The one vital report that came through but never reached the bridge was received at 9.40pm from the *Mesaba*: 'Ice reported in latitude 42 to 41°25' N, longitude 49 to 50°30' W. Saw much heavy pack ice and great number large icebergs. Also field ice.' This position she gave was right ahead of us and not many miles distant. That he received the message is known, and it was read by the other operator in his bunk. The operator who received it was busy at the time working wireless messages to and from Cape Race, also with his accounts, and he put the message under a paperweight at his elbow, just until he squared up what he was doing and he would then have brought it to the bridge. That delay proved fatal and was the main cause of the loss of that magnificent ship and hundreds of lives.

He then comments that you would have to be uncomfortably close to an iceberg to actually 'smell' ice, although in the early part of his biography he quotes an old sea dog who did in fact claim to 'smell' ice.

Great Uncle Bertie also mentions in his book that, at one point, he and Murdoch were standing on the bridge chatting together on that fateful night and were remarking between themselves how steady the ship was with an absence of any vibration; something that is not only completely at odds with Lawrence Beesley's comments about vibration from the ship's engines but is also not in line with other remarks by passengers. My great uncle states that:

> We were making an easy 22 knots. If there had been either wind or swell the berg would have been rendered visible through the water breaking at its base.

He also adds an endorsement:

> Captain E. J. (Smith) was one of the ablest skippers on the Atlantic... went down and was lost with the ship and so escaped that never-to-be-forgotten ordeal carried out in Washington: repeated again in England and finally concluded in the Law Courts.

Titanic's first disaster

The First Class passenger list of the *Titanic* read like an extract from the American rich list and included names like Guggenheim, Struss, Astor and of course the 'unsinkable Molly Brown'. But as the giant liner was leaving Southampton harbour the wash from her great hull, propelled by the turning of her twin thirty-eight-ton propellers, produced a suction so powerful that a much smaller liner, the *New York*, moored at the quayside was drawn towards the *Titanic* with such gigantic force that she broke free from her moorings and moved in an apparently unstoppable course towards the bigger ship. Somehow Captain Smith was able to issue the rapid orders that avoided a collision, thus managing for once to avoid adding to his existing list of mercantile casualties. Not a good omen for the start of an 'unsinkable' liner's maiden voyage!

Before the ship had travelled very much further there was a request to Second Officer Lightoller from one of the lookouts at the ship's stem and also from two in the crow's nest for missing binoculars. My great uncle told them that he would attend to it, as he knew binoculars had been available during the so-called 'sea trials' on Belfast Lough. However, as we have seen, Third Officer Blair had left the ship with the keys to the relevant locker. Yet Lightoller seemed surprisingly unconcerned by the situation, saying that binoculars could be purchased when they reached New York – a promise he would never be able to fulfil. Just one more act of carelessness in the running of the most expensive and most luxurious ship ever built. Or could there possibly have been some other reason for Great Uncle Bertie's apparent lack of interest in something so vital to the safety of the *Titanic* as the required pairs of binoculars?

Wealthy people a hundred years ago were just as consumed with guarding their riches as they are today, and a ship carrying a collection of America's rich and very rich meant that many of them would be concerned with the state of their stocks and shares on the world's leading exchanges. Thus the *Titanic*'s wireless operators were kept almost constantly busy receiving the latest prices for their pampered clients in the luxury of the liner's First Class staterooms and suites. Without attention being taken up by the literally hundreds of message being transmitted and received on behalf of these rich investors, better contact could have been made and maintained with potential rescuers.

Lightoller reads the stars

Sometime between seven and 7.30pm on Sunday April 14th 1912, my great uncle, Second Officer Lightoller, left the bridge for his supper break. On returning he noticed an almost completely dark sky, a number of stars, and most importantly a sharp drop of some four degrees in the air temperature while he had been absent. He summoned Pitman, the Third Officer, to assist him in calculating the ship's exact position. As he watched the stars with his sextant, he shouted to Pitman who would take a reading from the ship's clock, kept in a special box on the bridge for this particular procedure. Pitman then set to in the chart room to calculate with various tables the exact position of the ship, based on the celestial bodies and the timings shouted to him by the Second Officer.

In fact, these positionings were later found to be inaccurate, resulting in rescuers heading for the *Titanic* ending up some way away from the actual disaster area. No one has ever conclusively apportioned blame for this disastrous error. It could have been Pitman's calculations, or perhaps Great Uncle Bertie misread the stars. Just one more blunder to add to the list of contributory factors in the loss of so many lives.

Bertie is confused

My great uncle's autobiography contains an extraordinary and mind-boggling inaccuracy. It reads: 'The time we struck was 2.20am April 12th of tragic memory.'

At the time of writing his autobiography, *Titanic and Other Ships*, my great uncle was just over sixty and it would be another eighteen years before I attended his funeral at Mortlake crematorium. Although there are passages in his book that are not of the greatest literary merit, I have no recall of his being in his dotage when he wrote the book. How then could he have so patently got both the time and the date of the collision wrong? This was surely the most memorable event of his entire life. If he got this wrong, what else did he get wrong in his recalling of the tragedy, not only in his own book, but in his testimonies and statements that followed the disaster? Surely Great Aunt Sylvia would have spotted this kind of glaring error? I know that, when I spent time with her, some twenty years later, she was extremely 'on the ball'. Anyway, this passage in my great uncle's book continues:

> ...it was about ten minutes later that the Fourth Officer, Boxhall, opened my door and seeing me awake said: 'We've hit an iceberg... the water is up to F deck in the mail room.' The decks in a modern liner are lettered from the boat deck down. A, B, C, D, E and so on. The fact of the water having reached F deck showed she was badly holed but, at the time, although I knew it was serious, I had not thought that it was likely to prove fatal.

Lightoller is full of praise (rather overzealous praise) for the *Titanic*'s crew and their capabilities in the face of extreme danger and disaster:

> You may be sure that the crew of the *Titanic* had been put through a fine sieve and particular care taken that there were no misfits. The result was that when the call came – not a call of bugles, but the call on every man to exhibit the highest

individual effort, intelligence and courage, the response was
absolutely universal – not a man failed!

This is a superb example of overblown Edwardian high-class
jingoistic verbiage, reading more like something penned by a
literate corporate official than by a working sailor who had left
school at thirteen, embarking on a life at sea with no chance of
further education. It compares very strangely with the rough-
and-ready style of much else in Great Uncle Bertie's
autobiography. Earlier passages in his book are couched in the
language of an ordinary seafaring man and seem more of a fit
than much of the Second Officer's trumpeting description of
the collision. For instance, an earlier passage states:

My first voyage, horribly seasick – and sick of the sea... At
long last, clear of the Chops of the Channel, we squared away
to a fine Nor'-Nor'-West breeze and tore down through the
Roaring Forties towards good old 'flying fish' weather.

And again:

We rigged up stump t'gallant masts in Rio for the simple
reason, I suppose, they had no spars long enough for t'gallant,
royal and skysail masts.

Lightoller's description of how the *Titanic* came to be so badly
damaged casts aspersions upon both the design and build of
the great ship. However, his theories in these respects did not
appear to surface during either the American or British
inquiries into the sinking. He is quite clear in his
autobiography where the structural blame lay:

She struck the berg well forward of the foremast and evidently
there had been a slight shelf protruding below the water. This
pierced her bow as she threw her whole weight on the ice,
some actually falling on her foredeck. The impact flung her
bow off, but only by the whip and spring of the ship. Again,
she struck, this time a little further aft: each blow stove in a

plate below the water line as the ship had no inherent strength to resist.

What really happened?

Arriving in New York on the maiden voyage of the *Olympic*, well before her 'twin' the *Titanic* was launched, Bruce Ismay proudly faced the press to puff the magnificence of his latest 'Sovereign of the Seas'. Asked by the *New York Times* about the cost of such a piece of magnificence he replied: '...with furniture, fittings and such, $10 million.' How did Ismay and the White Star Line come to spend that sort of money on their ships?

In the building of the *Titanic*, three thousand men laboured for two years on the ship before her launch, by which time she had cost the company seven-and-a-half million dollars (the likely cost of building such a ship today would exceed four hundred million dollars). She was larger than many a World War Two aircraft carrier! Yet the three million rivets used in her construction still couldn't hold her together. This was before the days of arc welding, and the one-inch-thick iron plates for the ship's hull were obviously not thick enough to withstand the kind of impact that sank her on her first voyage.

Great Uncle Bertie obviously agreed, because he continues:

Had it been, for instance, the old *Majestic* or even the *Oceanic*, the chances are that either of them would have been strong enough to take a blow and be bodily thrown off without serious damage.

So my great uncle was of the opinion that this wondrous ship, on which he was a senior officer, was not really capable of withstanding a blow in the same way that older ships of the line might. Why did this not come out in his testimonies to both the US Senate Inquiry and the one held by the Board of Trade in London? He was surely not a forgetful man, yet what he left unsaid at the inquiries would fill a book.

Chapter 18
Lady Louise reveals all

A family secret

My second cousin, Lady Louise Patten, claims to have uncovered a most extraordinary omission on her grandfather's part, which she says was only revealed to her by her grandmother, my Great Aunt Sylvia, after the great man's death. It was so memorable and so glaring an omission that it remained a family secret until second cousin Louise decided to finally mention it in her book *Good as Gold*. These extracts from an interview she gave to the *Oxford Times* on October 14th 2010 are startlingly revealing:

Lady Louise Patten... is not only the granddaughter of the great hero of the *Titanic* tragedy, but is the last person alive to know what really happened on the night the *Titanic* sank... Lady Patten (as she became following her husband's ennoblement) has decided the time has come to reveal facts about SS *Titanic* known within her family for almost a century, about which she has remained silent for four decades.

She learnt from her grandmother, the wife of Commander Charles Herbert Lightoller, what really happened between the sighting of the iceberg at 11.36pm on Sunday April 14th 1912 and the final shutting down of the engines at 12.15am on Monday the 15th...

The key claim she makes is that the liner struck the iceberg because of a basic steering blunder, not because the liner was travelling too fast or the failure to spot the massive berg in time, as the world has continued to believe... In a catastrophic mistake, the helmsman simply turned the wrong way, with a basic misunderstanding of orders resulting in the *Titanic* steaming towards the iceberg instead of away...

'Four people knew the truth about the collision,' argues Lady Patten, 'three of whom were lost with the ship. Captain Smith, Chief Officer Wilde and First Officer Murdoch... My grandfather was the only senior officer left alive, and the sole survivor who knew precisely why *Titanic* had foundered...'

Having kept the family secret for so long, the former management consultant... has chosen to reveal it in a surprising way. For the disclosures are threaded through the plot of Lady Patten's latest novel *Good as Gold*... The bombshell, securing massive publicity for the novel, comes at the end of the book in an eight-page afterword...

'*Titanic* sailed during the transition from sail to steam. Two different systems were in operation to communicate the steering of ships: Rudder Orders, used for steam ships, and Tiller Orders, used for sailing ships. Crucially, the two steering systems were the complete opposite of one another. So a command to turn "hard a-starboard" meant turn the wheel right under one system and left under the other...'

Confusion at the wheel

Helmsman Robert Hitchins was new to the North Atlantic, where Tiller Orders were still in use. When First Officer Murdoch spotted the iceberg, his "hard a-starboard" order was disastrously misinterpreted by Hitchins... 'The steersman panicked and reverted to Rudder Orders. The reason why *Titanic* hit the iceberg... is because he turned the wheel the wrong way...'

... a dramatic final meeting of the four senior officers took place in the First Officer's cabin shortly before the *Titanic* went down. Lightoller heard not only about the fatal mistake but about a decision, made afterwards, that sealed the fate of the ship and its passengers. Bruce Ismay, chairman of *Titanic*'s owner the White Star Line, persuaded Captain Smith to continue sailing.

'To turn the wrong way was a blunder but my grandfather described the decision to try to keep the *Titanic* moving forward after the collision as criminal... The nearest ship was four hours away. Had she remained "stop", it is probable that *Titanic* would have floated until help arrived. Greed and pride were lethal motivators... Nearly forty years later, with granny and my mother long dead, I was plotting my second novel... My grandfather's extraordinary experiences felt like perfect material for *Good as Gold...*'

Her grandfather, who died shortly before she was born, was the only man able to reveal the shocking truth to the inquiry into the disaster. Lady Patten puts his silence down to a code of honour, which made him feel duty bound to protect his employer White Star Line. 'It was all about *Titanic*'s insurance policy,' she argues.

'It was made clear to him by those at the top that if the company were found to be negligent, it would be bankrupted and every job would be lost. The enquiry had to be a whitewash.'

Now this appears to be a revelation of extraordinary magnitude. There could be no reason for my second cousin, Lady Louise, as the wife of a Member of Parliament and Knight of the Realm, to be anything other than truthful in her revelation of her grandmother's secret. Thus, if Great Uncle Bertie withheld such valuable information at the inquiries into the sinking, made no comment about the inadequate structure of the ship's build and was generally evasive and unhelpful, particularly at the US inquiry, what else might he have been hiding?

More lies?

Louise Patten in her interview mentions a meeting between the four senior officers, Smith, Wilde, Murdoch and Lightoller, that took place in the First Officer's cabin shortly before the *Titanic* went down. What did they discuss? Was it how to close ranks at an inevitable inquiry? Or was it something even more secret than that?

Had something happened that involved an even bigger lie than the ones I have so far managed to untangle from this web of maritime subterfuge? After all, my great uncle, the only senior surviving officer of the disaster, spent time cloistered in a private cabin with Bruce Ismay on board the *Carpathia*, as it carried the *Titanic* survivors towards the port of New York. What did those two men talk about? How did this conversation, like the one between Ismay and the other officers in the stricken ship, influence an upright and ostensibly honest officer of the highly regarded White Star Line to falsify and fabricate his testimonies before a group of worthy US senators and highly qualified nautical men in London?

So why did my Great Uncle Bertie, who had heroically refused to leave the sinking ship on one of the last two lifeboats and who supposedly 'went down with the ship', hide what he knew of the real reasons for the disaster? According to his testimony published in the *Christian Science Monitor*, God, he believed, rather than pure luck had helped him to survive, plunging him first into the depths but bringing him to the surface again where he was able to climb onto an upturned lifeboat and thus save himself – surely a true resurrection. So did the *Titanic* really open up like a tin can, with an iceberg as the tin-opener?

What a waste of all those millions of dollars! No binoculars; a risk-taking Captain; Great Uncle Bertie, the only surviving senior officer, omitting vital information in his testimonies to official inquiries, at which he was noticeably unhelpful. What was going on? Theories and myths, conspiracies and fantasies surround the sinking of the *Titanic* to this day.

Unanswered questions

When I first came across the box of *Titanic* press clippings in Grandma Gertrude's house, I felt unable to admit my discovery to her. However, the idea of this great ship sinking stayed with me and grew in my imagination until, some time after Great Uncle Bertie's death in 1952, I felt able to broach the subject. Grandma Gertrude was by then well into her eighties but as bright as a button.

'Your great uncle left the *Titanic*.' This meant nothing to me at the time; but later, when I came across the Second Officer's oft-quoted remark that followed the sinking, 'I didn't leave the ship – the ship left me!', I began to wonder if my grandmother had misquoted her brother, or whether perhaps she meant something more revealing by her remark. So, one day when Grandma Gertrude and I were alone, I tentatively raised the subject; a subject I was now longing to hear more about – my great uncle's part in the most famous maritime tragedy: the sinking of a nation's hopes for transatlantic supremacy.

'Your Great Uncle Bertie was a company man. He did as he was told. He was an officer but he didn't run the company.'

I wondered then, and still wonder, what exactly she meant by this and just how much she knew of the machinations surrounding the short and, in the end, inglorious life of what had promised to be the biggest and the best of all Atlantic liners.

True and false stories

The supposed details of the fatal collision with an iceberg, the heroism and the histrionics, the lack of both lifeboats and lifeboat drill, the great ship rising up in the dark ocean like an enormous whale preparing to dive down into the depths – each survivor had a different story to tell.

There are also bizarre urban legends that have grown up around the sinking, like the one propounded by the rumour-mongering website, Snopes.com. Their piece begins by retelling the story of the uncanny resemblance between Morgan Robertson's 1898 novella *Futility, or the Wreck of the Titan* and the *Titanic*'s sinking. An ill omen if ever there was one, but obviously J. Bruce Ismay and all at the White Star Line were either not avid readers of this kind of book or were else too thick-skinned to take the hint. Snopes.com's piece then continues:

A much lesser known – but no less remarkable – coincidence is that, at the very moment that the *Titanic* struck an iceberg in the North Atlantic, late on the evening of April 14th 1912, the film *The Poseidon Adventure* – a movie about the desperate efforts of a group of passengers to survive the sinking of an ocean liner – was being screened aboard ship... The White Star Line, proudly dedicated to sparing no expense in ensuring that its new flagship *Titanic* provided every luxury their passengers could desire, did not overlook this still relatively novel one. The *Titanic* carried its own projector and a complement of movies rented from the British office of a US film distributor.

This passage further suggests that, as films were in their infancy and retained a rather sleazy image, they were shown after 11pm and that this timing also allowed the ship's orchestra to accompany the films, having by that late hour discharged their duties in the ship's ballroom. The website then states that this earlier version of *The Poseidon Adventure* ran an amazing fifty-three minutes and was directed by the great D. W. Griffith, no less, creator of the most expensive and controversial film of the time, *Birth of a Nation*.

Snopes.com has managed to fool a considerable number of people with this story. An urban myth, tailor-made for the wish-fulfilment of romantics everywhere, it is in fact an excellently designed con. Paul Gallico wrote a short novella in 1969 about a cruise ship turning turtle and trapping a glorious cross-section of human flotsam in its upturned hull. Hollywood subsequently grabbed the idea in 1972, during an era when studios were hooked on the success of disaster movies like *Towering Inferno*. Those of us old enough to have seen the seventies film of *Poseidon*, or young enough to have caught it on late night repeats, will probably remember what a great adventure movie it was. The public and the media in general have always been drawn to the tale of the *Titanic*, which is why numerous rumours like the *Poseidon Adventure* story have sprung up over the years.

Because of the magnitude and the horror of the *Titanic*'s sinking, many people have continued to search for the truth about how and why this terrible event occurred and why no one was brought to book over it. Was J. Bruce Ismay an arrogant fool or was he something worse – a totally ruthless capitalist, cast in the same mould as his ultimate ruler, the merciless and avaricious J. Pierpont Morgan?

My task has really been to satisfy my own intense curiosity about this event – one that took place many years before I was born, but which not only involved my great uncle, an extraordinary figure whom I had met as a child and had been encouraged to view as a national hero, but also had caused incredible ripples to be set in motion by the magnitude of the event and which continued to spread in ever widening circles throughout both sides of my family. However, my search for the truth, if it could ever be told, has led me down countless alleyways of half-truths, legends, conspiracy theories and distorted facts. As Walter Lord in his hugely successful book of the sinking, *A Night to Remember*, remarks:

> It is a rash man, indeed, who would set himself up as final arbiter on all that happened the incredible night the *Titanic* went down.

The public's insatiable appetite for records of death and destruction has been well fed by the media for the past hundred years; and the writer Joseph Conrad, himself a seasoned mariner like my great uncle, wrote of his feelings about the sensationalising of a tragedy like that of the *Titanic*:

> It is with a certain bitterness that one must admit to oneself that the late SS *Titanic* had a 'good press'. It is perhaps because I have no great practice of daily newspapers (I have never seen so many of them together lying about my room), that the white spaces and the big lettering of the headlines have an

incongruously festive air to my eyes, a disagreeable effect of a
feverish exploitation of the sensational God-send. And if ever
a loss at sea fell under the definition, in the terms of a bill of
lading, of Act of God, this one does, in its magnitude,
suddenness and severity; and in the chastening influence it
should have on the self-confidence of mankind.

Those caught up in this most terrible of disasters, whether
survivors or bereaved, would bear the emotional scar-tissue for
as long as they lived. And those, like my grandmother, who
lost neither friends nor family in the sinking, would still have
to live with a series of unanswered questions concerning the
event – questions that could never be fully answered. The
endless imagining and guesswork still goes on, half a century
after Second Officer Lightoller passed away and, plagued by
half-truths and shadowy theories, I still seem very little nearer
to the complete truth of what happened in the North Atlantic
sea on that awful night all those long years ago.

Did the helmsman really make a fatal mistake in turning
the wheel the wrong way, resulting in a mammoth loss of life?
My second cousin Louise Patten certainly maintains that this
is true. Even more importantly, if my great uncle could lie
about more than one thing, what else even more shocking
might he have been hiding from the world?

More conflicting stories

There is considerable difference of opinion among testimonies
of survivors as to whether the *Titanic* actually broke in half
before sinking. Certainly Lawrence Beesley maintained that
the ship rose to the perpendicular, before plunging straight
down in one piece. When oceanic explorers were finally able to
view the wrecked ship from a submersible in 1985, they found
the liner in two halves. However, it is generally agreed that
plunging twelve-and-a-half thousand feet with a weight of
forty-six thousand tons would easily have split the ship in half
with the impact of hitting the sea bed. The question of whether
or not the *Titanic* broke in two before sliding beneath the

waves is of some importance as, if this were indeed the case, it may throw some light on the actual strength or otherwise of the seams that held the ship together. Certainly Great Uncle Bertie cast aspersions upon the ultimate strength of the steel plates that made up *Titanic*'s hull and the riveting that held them in place.

It has been stated by experts in various documents since the tragedy that it was the extreme cold of the North Atlantic that would have rapidly extinguished life, rather than actual drowning in a calm sea and clad in life jackets. However, Lawrence Beesley in his book *The Loss of the SS Titanic* presents us with a heart-rending account from the viewpoint of survivors in the lifeboats, which is directly at odds with the suggestion of multiple rapid deaths from freezing:

> Unprepared as we were for such a thing, the cries of the drowning floating across the quiet sea filled us with stupefaction. We longed to return and rescue at least some of the drowning, but we knew it was impossible. The boat was filled to standing-room and to return would mean the swamping of us all and so the Captain-Stoker told his crew to row away from the cries... think of it! A few more boats, a few more planks of wood nailed together in a particular way at a trifling cost and all those men and women whom the world can so ill-afford to lose would be with us today, there would be no mourning in thousands of homes which now are desolate and these words need not have been written.

A moving and eloquent account of a tragedy that might, for a number of reasons, have been so easily averted. However, we know from various reports, both from survivors and the captain and crew of the rescue ship, *Carpathia*, that a number of *Titanic*'s lifeboats were only half full or, in some cases, carrying as few as fourteen people. Why did boats that had room for more not pick up some of the poor souls crying for help in the freezing Atlantic water? The first excuse for hurrying away from the ship was the fear of suction as she went down, but we know there was none. The more likely reason is, I'm afraid, that *in extremis* self-preservation grips most humans more strongly than a desire to save their fellows.

Jumping ship

What did Joseph Conrad's *Lord Jim* have in common with J. Bruce Ismay and Charles Herbert Lightoller? If one considers the life of the writer Joseph Conrad and that of Commander Lightoller, ex-Second Officer of the White Star Line's ill-fated superliner, the *Titanic*, they had more in common than the mere fact of both being seafaring men.

Conrad's anti-hero Jim is supposedly based on a true incident involving a young sailor, Augustine Podmore Williams. He was one of the crew on a ship, the *Jeddah*, carrying Muslim pilgrims from Singapore to Jeddah in 1880 when, encountering extreme bad weather, the ship began to flounder. Williams, thinking the vessel was about to sink, jumped ship without making any serious attempt to rescue the thousands of pilgrims on board. He made his escape in a lifeboat, together with the captain and his wife. Williams and the captain were astounded, on reaching Aden, to discover that the *Jeddah* had in fact not sunk, but had been towed to safety with all aboard saved from a watery grave. Williams merely received a reprimand for dereliction of duty, and is understood to have gone on to lead a happy and fruitful life; whereas Conrad's *Lord Jim* remains obsessed with his having jumped ship and, consumed with guilt, spends the rest of his life obsessively seeking to prove himself a hero. Conrad's Jim dreams of becoming 'an example of devotion to duty as unfailingly as a hero in a book'.

In the Wordsworth Classics Edition of *Lord Jim*, Susan Jones in her excellent and erudite introduction points out that in this, as in his other novel *Heart of Darkness*, Conrad 'shows the gap between extreme forms of idealism and the necessity of responding to real situations of life'.

Thus, an interesting comparison could be drawn between Lightoller and Ismay, two men who each in his own fashion 'jumped' from the stricken *Titanic*. Joseph Bruce Ismay jumped into a lifeboat reserved for women and children, while Second Officer Charles Herbert Lightoller jumped into the freezing Atlantic, just as the fatally wounded liner was about to plunge to her watery grave. Instinctive self-preservation was evident in both instances.

Ismay's guilt appears to have dogged him to his dying day, based on more than just that one instinctive act of self preservation; whereas Lightoller, possibly aware of the many contributory elements to the tragedy, went on to be not only feted as a hero of that dreadful night, but highly commended for his bravery in both World War I and World War II. Would Mary Baker Eddy's Calvinistic father have questioned as to whether Ismay was 'Bad' and Lightoller 'Good?' Or was the apparently blameless Lightoller forced by an unscrupulous superior to divert from what should have been an honest account of the disaster to a devious and palpably dishonest testimony in the harsh light of the subsequent official inquiries?

If we can absolve the *Titanic*'s Second Officer of insufficient scrupulousness in the testing of the lifeboats during the Belfast Lough sea trials, and even the subsequent cover-up of the helmsman's fatal error, as described by my second cousin, Lady Louise Patten; and if we discount the possibility of Lightoller's possible faulty reading of the stars producing an inexact position of the ship prior to the collision, there may be other transgressions of an even more serious nature that we should not overlook.

Chapter 19
The drama of the *Olympic*

Leading actors in the drama

The world knows of the sins of Joseph Bruce Ismay, who to many remains the evil owner of the doomed *Titanic*. He carried to his grave the cries of the dying and drowning passengers who perished on his 'unsinkable' ship – a floating hotel of preposterous luxury and extravagant elegance – Ismay's ego on the ocean!

However, of the senior surviving officer, Charles Herbert Lightoller, most people know little or nothing A highly experienced sailor who had been at sea since the age of thirteen, he was hailed as a hero many times over: once for saving lives as the *Titanic* sank on her maiden voyage; once for allegedly shooting down a German Zeppelin airship in World War I; once for putting a German submarine out of action by ramming it; once for acting as a spy in World War II; and once for racing back and forth across the English Channel, together with his wife, Sylvia, in their small motor yacht to the beaches of Dunkirk to rescue the British troops trapped there under heavy German artillery fire.

The shooting

There is no doubt that senior officers on the *Titanic* were issued with revolvers and ammunition, once the seriousness of the situation became truly apparent to all concerned. In James

Cameron's film, *Titanic*, one of the ship's officers, and it is suggested that it is First Officer Murdoch, is seen shooting one or more passengers before then turning the gun on himself.

Reports, conversations and rumours regarding an officer on the *Titanic* shooting himself circulated on the rescue ship, *Carpathia*, before she even reached New York. However, these sources are many and varied and the press lost no time in picking up on them, embellishing the stories as they saw fit.

In the *New York Times* of April 20th 1912, one of the surviving First Class passengers, Robert Williams Daniel, is quoted as saying that it was First Officer Murdoch who shot himself. In the *Washington Evening Star* on April 22nd 1912, a Second Class passenger, Miss Mary Davies, is also quoted as witnessing Murdoch commit suicide with a revolver. On the other hand, the April 19th edition of the *New York Times* quotes a certain Dr Dodge as saying that two men attempting to jump into a lifeboat reserved for women and children were shot by one or more officers. However, he makes no mention of Murdoch killing himself.

Many and varied are the stories – some apparently accurate, many merely hearsay – of the possible shooting of passengers and Murdoch turning his gun on himself. However, James Cameron, a self-confessed *Titanic* freak quite apart from being a truly great motion-picture author, is known to be a stickler for authenticity. Although the central love story of Jack and Rose, a steerage passenger and a society beauty from First Class, is pure fiction, most of the other events of the tragic night were meticulously researched. Therefore, the inclusion of the scene during the sinking when Murdoch shoots two Italians attempting to board a lifeboat reserved for women and children before killing himself may indeed have some veracity.

In his book *The Night Lives On*, Walter Lord, acclaimed author of *A Night to Remember*, quotes a letter published in the London *Daily Telegraph* and the *Daily Sketch*, purporting to be written by one of the survivors – an Irishman, Eugene

Patrick Daly – to his sister, in which he mentions an officer on the *Titanic* killing himself after shooting two men dead.

Anyone who, after the event, suggested that the scene on the sinking ship towards the end was anything other than total chaos was misinformed, or else they misremembered. The important thing about the possible shooting incident, which has particularly intrigued writers and commentators for a hundred years, is that the truth will never be known. And it must therefore be accepted that under extreme duress men (and women) are capable of both heroic and seemingly despicable acts. Great Uncle Bertie was always at great pains to stress that First Officer Murdoch died like a hero and a gentleman. But then, the Commander was somewhat economical with the truth on several counts, apparently to save the good name of the owners and officers of the *Titanic* – not least of all Second Officer Charles Herbert Lightoller.

The strange case of the *Olympic*

However, there is one book that for me stands out from the rest. This deals with a possible conspiracy on the part of the owners, executives and officers of the *Titanic*. If there are indeed any truly credible elements to this theory, it would mean that my great uncle was involved in something that neither his widow, my Great Aunt Sylvia, nor his sister, my Grandma Gertrude, could possibly find easy to accept. The book in question is Robin Gardiner's *The Titanic Conspiracy*.

On June 14th 1911, the brand new liner *Olympic*, the first of the White Star Line's proposed trio of superliners, sailed from Southampton on her first voyage to New York under Captain Edward John Smith. She arrived on the fifth day of her crossing but, as she was docking, collided with the tug *O. L. Holenbeck*, causing the much smaller vessel considerable damage. Three months later, on September 20th, *Olympic* again set forth from Southampton to cross the Atlantic. This time, Captain Smith tangled with something rather larger than a tug: it was the 7,350-ton naval cruiser, HMS *Hawke*.

Both vessels were severely damaged in the collision and *Olympic* required two weeks' repair work by her original builders, Harland and Wolff. The damage to *Olympic* above the water line was very noticeable. However, further damage, only visible when the ship was in dry dock, was very considerable. The *Hawke*, like many of the Royal Navy's cruisers at the time, was built with a steel battering ram just below the water line at her bows. The result was that it punched a hole approximately twenty-five feet by ten feet in the liner. Also, one of *Olympic*'s turbine engines had been put out of commission by the collision. On September 22nd an official Royal Naval Inquiry was convened to discover the cause of the accident. As is usual under such circumstances, only naval personnel were called to give evidence and the judgement of the president of the inquiry, Sir Samuel Evans, was that: '...the collision was solely due to faulty navigation of the *Olympic*.'

No money for White Star

The White Star Line appealed but, although they eventually took the matter all the way to the House of Lords, they received no recompense whatsoever.

As good fortune would have it, the collision between the two ships occurred at lunchtime, which meant that most of *Olympic*'s passengers were in the dining room, rather than in their cabins, many of which on the Second Class deck were destroyed. Thus no loss of life occurred as a result of the 'accident'.

Robin Gardiner is a writer with a lifelong interest in the *Titanic* and the mysteries surrounding her sinking. In his book *The Great Titanic Conspiracy* he suggests that the great liner's collision with HMS *Hawke* was no accident. He supports his theory by pointing out that Commander Blunt, in charge of HMS *Hawke* at the time of it ramming *Olympic*, received no kind of reprimand for his part in the affair, although he must have contributed to it. In fact, he was rewarded by being given command of a larger cruiser.

At the time of the accident, crews of merchant vessels were hired for one passage at a time; so that, on a transatlantic trip, a seaman would be hired and paid to sail from Southampton to New York and return to Southampton again. However, after the damaged *Olympic* had been inspected by Harland and Wolff's specialists, White Star announced that the ship was declared a 'wreck' and thus, under the terms of the crew's contracts, no one would be paid for the voyage to America and back. Those crew members booked to sail *Olympic* to New York took their grievances to the Court of Appeal. However, as the accident had already been judged by the naval inquiry to be entirely the fault of the owners, there would only be one reason for the ship's owners to withhold the crew's wages – *Olympic* was a 'wreck'!

Patching up *Olympic*

Olympic was given a gigantic patch, made of wood above the water line and steel plates below, at Harland and Wolff's repair yard at Southampton. The ship had two engines, one at port and one at starboard but, as the starboard one was out of commission since the collision, the ship steamed back to Harland and Wolff's main shipyard in Belfast under just her port engine. But it seems as though the 'patching up job' failed, as before she could reach Belfast the same two compartments of the hull damaged in the collision with the *Hawke* were again filled with water.

Conspiracies the world over

In a 2008 global poll of seventeen countries, only forty-six per cent of those surveyed believed al-Qaeda was responsible for the collapse of the twin towers of New York's World Trade Centre in 2001. That means that an amazing fifty-four per cent of people around the world thought it was either masterminded by George W. Bush and his advisors or other interested parties. The US certainly had good reason to invade Iraq, for the Western world had wanted to regain control of Middle Eastern oil for many years. The most common conspiracy theory surrounds the possibility of controlled demolition of the twin towers in the same way that explosives are sited in the foundations of a building to bring it straight down, as in the images of the collapsing twin towers seen on TV by millions around the world.

However, this is not to say that the Bush administration actually destroyed 2,998 lives to justify invading someone else's country. Similarly, conspiracy theories surrounding the loss of the *Titanic* do not necessarily prove a deliberate sinking. Nevertheless, like the collapsing of the twin towers, the sinking of the *Titanic* is worth careful scrutinising, as there is always the possibility of a major conspiracy and one that through bad planning and inept execution caused the unintentional loss of over fifteen hundred lives. Robin Gardiner and others have unearthed some compelling facts about both the *Olympic* and the *Titanic*, concerning events influenced by Britain's pathological fear of a powerful German empire ready to mount an invasion of Western Europe and even Britain.

Who will carry the troops?

Let us consider the first of the possible conspiracies that may have contributed to that most famous of sinking of all. *Titanic* was a British-registered liner, but one that was ultimately owned by the American multimillionaire J. Pierpont Morgan through his multinational conglomerate, International Mercantile Marine. The British government had funded the Cunard company's liners, partly to restore Britain's prestige in transatlantic travel but also because these ships were part of the Army and Navy's plan to turn them into armoured cruisers or troop carriers in the likelihood of an aggressive move by the warlike Germany. Carrying troops to wherever they were required in the world was a prime requisite for the defence of Britain and its Empire. However, the Cunard liners had not stood up well to tests by the Navy; and possibly a deliberate ramming of the *Olympic* could also have been a test of the White Star's ship to see what its capabilities were under attack. Like the Cunard ships, she obviously didn't stand up to the test of being rammed by a naval cruiser.

Chapter 20
It's all about money

Priceless artefacts

The plot thickens when we consider the following. Although the tomb of the ancient Egyptian ruler Tutankhamen was officially opened in November 1922, it seems likely that Lord Carnarvon and the explorer Howard Carter had been plundering the tomb for more than ten years prior to this. Some of the materials removed appeared to be in the form of papyrus scrolls. One of these was of monumental significance. It suggested a reworking of the second book of the Bible, *Exodus*, and recorded that the Jews were not God's chosen people but merely a mixed race of Egyptians and slaves. In the wrong hands this document had the very real possibility of destroying the foundation of the Christian and Jewish religions.

In 1912, J. P. Morgan paid eighty thousand pounds for this Coptic scroll. He was well aware of the political and religious value of its contents, having made it his life's work, on the back of his multimillion-pound business empire, to travel the world seeking Christian-Judaic artefacts of all kinds. Fearing an invasion of Britain by the aggressive Kaiser, J. P. Morgan began shipping his extremely valuable rarities out of Britain and across the Atlantic to the safety of New York's Museum of Modern Art. The precious Coptic scroll was to be one of these items.

Did the British government become aware of the projected loss of this inflammatory scroll? Would its publication have caused cataclysmic uprisings and unrest in the Middle East affecting, as now, Britain and America's control of vital oil sources for the West? Could an ancient parchment-like piece of papyrus rock the foundations of mighty religions and political empires? Anything is possible in those fragile worlds; but the sinking of a White Star liner that might have been carrying this vital Coptic scroll, bought by the fabulously wealthy preserver of Judeo-Christian artefacts – surely not? Yet, stranger things have happened.

Losing money hand over fist

A large and expensive liner like the *Olympic*, costing a fortune to repair – or even beyond repair – and with no redress from the British government or the Royal Navy for the great hole rent in her side: now that was a major financial problem for the White Star Line.

We know that the White Star Line had declared the *Olympic* a technical 'wreck' in order to avoid paying the crew for the transatlantic voyage curtailed by the collision with HMS *Hawke*. However, if White Star took the *Olympic* out of service, the company was going to be left with a huge deficit. In November 1911, the *Olympic* resumed her career at sea, with repairs made by using *Titanic*'s main propeller and shaft to replace the one damaged in the *Hawke* collision.

Olympic and *Titanic*, the two floating centrepieces of the White Star Line's seagoing collection, were reckoned to be the largest and most luxurious vessels of their time. Unfortunately, there are now some doubts as to their ultimate safety and seaworthiness.

Problem with the rivets

Much of the plating used to make up the hulls of the sister ships *Olympic* and *Titanic* was held in place by a new technique of hydraulic riveting, as opposed to the old-established system where red-hot rivets were hammered into place. It has been suggested that the instituting of a new form of labour-saving riveting was regarded by some of the shipyard workers as a possible threat to their jobs and certainly their wages. Whether this was the cause of the new form of riveting being poorly used is speculation, but it does seem as though the rivets used, and the holes prepared for them, were jobs often poorly done, resulting in large sections of the riveting failing within weeks of *Olympic* returning to service; and so the ship was again dry-docked for repairs in February 1912.

Photographs of the *Titanic* in Southampton shortly before her maiden voyage show a large area of her hull apparently repainted, but with paint that doesn't quite match the rest of the ship. On May 29th 1911, *Olympic* was registered at 45,323.8 gross registered tons. *Titanic* was registered on March 25th 1912 at 46,328.57 gross registered tons.

The 'switch'

By a complex set of calculations, relating to the cubic contents forming the ship's registered tonnage, *Olympic* became *Titanic*. Yet there was only one month in which to convert the *Olympic* to the look of the *Titanic* and also alter the *Titanic* to resemble her sister ship, *Olympic*. The White Star Line would never have been allowed to register a ship at less than its true tonnage, and so certain additions were made to bring *Olympic* up to the necessary gross tonnage. Joseph Bruce Ismay insisted on fitting screens to A Deck, so that First Class passengers promenading there should be sheltered. But who was going to go walking on deck in conditions so adverse that Atlantic waves would reach a deck fifty feet above the water?

James Cameron, obsessed with all things *Titanic*, managed to purchase a submersible vehicle with which he was able to dive twelve-and-a-half thousand feet to the wrecked *Titanic* on the bed of the North Atlantic Ocean. He was able to send a small robot camera on an extending arm into the wreck itself and thus film much of the interior. The robot was actually able to get inside a suite of rooms occupied by Ismay on the fateful voyage. Incredibly, the filming revealed the sitting room of Ismay's suite in a remarkable state of preservation, even after almost a hundred years beneath the sea. The stateroom included a cast-iron fireplace with marble surround. This particular veined marble is of a type where no two pieces ever have the same markings; yet photos of the marble fireplace in the wreck exactly match, not those of the *Titanic*, but pictures of Ismay's stateroom in the *Olympic* taken in 1911. Now this does beg the question – were the two ships switched? And why should the British and the American authorities fail to discover this or, even more worryingly, why did they cover up the switch if they knew about it?

My great uncle admitted in both his autobiography, *Titanic and Other Ships*, and in conversations with his wife, Great Aunt Sylvia, that he was part of a 'whitewash' when he went before the official inquiries into the sinking of the *Titanic*. But just how big a 'whitewash' was it?

Enter the Royal Navy

It was not until the year 2000 that the Royal Navy finally admitted that one of their ships – a cruiser, HMS *Sirius* – was actually in the area of the *Titanic*'s sinking the night it plunged to the bottom of the sea. Could this have been the 'mystery' ship that caused the dreadful damage to the *Titanic* and not an iceberg after all? In the two years leading up to the outbreak of World War I, both Britain and Germany were secretly patrolling both above and below the Atlantic. The British Navy, together with a number of interested parties, appear over the last hundred years or so to have harboured desires to raise the *Titanic* or at least gain access to the wreck. Why? Is it the reputed eight million pounds' worth of gold and other treasures that some claim went down with the ship? Of course, that would be about one billion pounds in today's money – quite an incentive.

The *Olympic* lives on

When American J. Pierpont Morgan decided to buy the company White Star Line, the British Government made no move to stop him, although they had subsidised Cunard in their successful bid for independence from the American corporate raider. However, their negotiations with Morgan stipulated that in the event of war with Germany, White Star Line ships would be made available as troop carriers or royal naval cruisers. And so it was that, in 1902, a deal was done. J. P. Morgan paid ten million pounds for the company, and Joseph Bruce Ismay became its managing director and chairman. Although the White Star Line was now part of Morgan's all-powerful IMM, an agreement was reached to build all the line's new ships at Harland and Wolff in Belfast. The *Olympic* had a long and illustrious career after the so-called *Titanic*'s sinking, including service as a troop ship during World War I.

On October 9th 1912, the White Star Line withdrew *Olympic* from service and returned her to Harland and Wolff's Belfast shipyard. Sixty-four wooden lifeboats were installed along the boat deck, an inner watertight skin was fitted to protect the engine and boiler rooms, and watertight bulkheads were extended upwards to B Deck.

The B Deck promenades, one of the few features that distinguished the *Olympic* from the *Titanic*, were removed to make room for additional cabins. In fact, the *Olympic* now looked incredibly like her lost sister ship, the *Titanic*.

The *Olympic* at war

This version of the *Olympic* proved to be a veritable warrior during the First World War, not only transporting over two hundred thousand troops, but equipped with twelve-pounder and 4.7-inch guns, ready to fight the enemy in any way she could. Early on the morning of May 12th 1918, the *Olympic*'s captain, Bertram Fox Hayes, sighted a German submarine, the U-103. As the *Olympic*'s guns were turned on the U-boat, it prepared to dive; but before it could do so, the big ship struck the submarine and part of its port propeller sliced through the U-boat's pressurised hull, forcing the German crew to immediately scuttle their submarine. The *Olympic* made no attempt to pick up survivors but left this job to the USS *Davies*. It was later revealed that the U-boat had been about to torpedo the *Olympic* but the liner had got in there first.

After World War I the *Olympic* returned to service as a luxury passenger liner and continued as such for many years afterwards, being constantly updated with the latest luxury fittings and equipment. That the *Olympic* remained so reliable and with such long-lived success, after the dreadful wounding it received from HMS *Hawke* in September 1911, seems somewhat improbable given the inevitable weakening of her hull by the cruiser's ramming. If indeed she sank in place of the *Titanic* on April 15th 1912, she would have only had some seven months in service following the mortal damage sustained in 1911. Perhaps seven months was about all the White Star Line could reasonably expect from a ship they had already declared a 'wreck'.

Reasons for the 'switch'

Olympic's collision with HMS *Hawke* was a major financial disaster for the White Star Line. Not only did it mean the loss of precious revenue from her scheduled sailings, but she was forced to return to Harland and Wolff's Belfast yards for extensive and costly repairs. At this point Ismay and the White Star Line announced that, as *Olympic*'s repairs were to be urgently carried out by Harland and Wolff, the completion of *Titanic* would have to be delayed. One reason given was that the *Olympic* had lost a propeller blade and so one had to be 'borrowed' from her sister ship, *Titanic*.

Five months later, *Olympic* again lost a propeller blade and was once more forced to 'borrow' from the almost-completed *Titanic*. Thus, as a result of *Olympic*'s damage and repair, the *Titanic*'s maiden voyage was delayed from March 20th 1912 to

April 10th 1912. Of course, all this losing of propeller blades and borrowing them from the *Titanic* may well have happened, and apparently the shedding of a blade by ships of this size was not unheard of a hundred years ago. Nevertheless, there does seem to have been a possible justification in the eyes of the *Olympic*'s owners for ditching her in mid Atlantic, claiming the insurance and being rid of an elegant liner that was fast beginning to look more like a troublesome old tub.

It was only when the *Olympic* was standing in dry dock at Harland and Wolff's yard, and her hull drained of all the water she'd taken in as a result of the collision with the *Hawke*, that the true extent of the damage to her could be estimated. Certainly a new crank, propshaft and propeller were needed, and the only way to obtain these and avoid a long wait for them was to borrow the ones currently waiting to be fitted to the sister ship *Titanic*. This would go a long way towards getting *Olympic* back into commission and earning money for her owners. However, the damage to one of the engines indicated that the centre line of the ship had been thrown out. As the patch on the *Olympic*'s hull that Harland and Wolff's Southampton repairers had attached did not hold, this was a further indication that the ship's hull was no longer rigid and would have to be stiffened. New bulkheads fitted longitudinally would help to rectify this problem.

Robert Ballard and the *Titanic*

Dr Robert Ballard is a very interesting man: a former US Navy officer much admired and highly experienced as an oceanographer. He has got close to some of the world's most important wrecks, including the German battleship *Bismarck*, the sunken liner *Lusitania* and John F. Kennedy's patrol boat, *PT-109*.

In the summer of 1985, Ballard began his search of the ocean bed for *Titanic*, an expedition financed by the US Navy. As Ballard had previously been successful in tracking down the wrecks of two nuclear-powered submarines that had sunk in the 1960s, they allowed him facilities to search for and explore the *Titanic*. It was the US Navy's way of saying 'thank you'. By 1986 Ballard had located the *Titanic* and descended in a submersible vehicle, enabling him to produce detailed photographic records of the *Titanic*'s condition. When he explored the wreck, Ballard discovered a bulkhead that did not appear on any of the vessel's design drawings.

The crankshaft and propeller shaft originally intended for *Titanic* were fitted as replacements to *Olympic* and the number was registered as '401'. This number is clearly visible in pictures taken of the wreck by Robert Ballard, indicating the extreme likelihood that the ship lying in 15,600 feet of North Atlantic water is in fact the *Olympic* and not the *Titanic*. Of course this raises the question of the marble fire surround in Ismay's *Titanic* cabin. If James Cameron's tiny robot camera showed conclusively that this was from the *Olympic*, how come Cameron failed to tell the world of this? There are several possible answers. Perhaps Cameron had reached a point of no return with his mammoth *Titanic* production and had no desire to scupper it. It could be that proper analyses of the shots of Ismay's *Titanic* stateroom were never undertaken until long after the film was completed. Who knows?

Part Four
Fraud and our hero

Chapter 21
A possible 'switch'

The reasons for the 'switch'

Until J. P. Morgan took over the White Star Line in 1901, J. Bruce Ismay had been the owner of the company. Now, Morgan's American multinational, IMM, had installed Ismay as Chairman and Managing Director – but the tune he had to dance to was J. P. Morgan's. Harland and Wolff could not afford to do a proper repair job on the *Olympic* without getting much of the up-front cost for this from the White Star Line. Meanwhile, White Star had a cash flow problem that J. P. Morgan, despite his excessive wealth, was not prepared to support.

So Ismay could see that, with the finishing of the *Titanic* delayed while repairs were carried out to the *Olympic*, plus the cost of these repairs, to say nothing of the lost revenue from *Olympic* being out of commission, everything added up to a looming financial crisis of huge proportions.

Maritime fraud

Apparently, the switching of vessels' identities is a fraud not unknown to insurance investigators. Experts have calculated that it would probably have taken longer to fully and properly repair the *Olympic* than dress *Titanic* up to look like her sister ship. Most importantly, both ships were built from the same set of plans.

Harland and Wolff announced that repairs to the *Olympic* were taking manpower and thus time from the completion of the *Titanic*, when in fact every second was being occupied with racing to carry out the huge cosmetic job of making *Olympic* look like *Titanic*. If this is indeed the route out of his troubles that Ismay decided to take, the big question is – was Great Uncle Bertie aware of the switch and, if so, at what point?

Having come directly from the White Star Line's *Oceanic*, Lightoller would never have sailed on the *Olympic*, and would therefore be unaware of the 'switch' until perhaps well into the maiden voyage. But my great uncle was a highly experienced sailor, for by the time he joined the ill-fated ship that he believed was the *Titanic*, although only thirty-three years of age, he was a rugged seaman who had survived storm and shipwreck on more than one occasion and therefore had a sailor's affinity with every ship he sailed in. Before the voyage had gone very far certain qualities about the ship must have alerted his suspicion that all was not well aboard this great 'new' liner.

For instance, one of the snags about the swapping of the two ships was that the starboard engine and shaft would vibrate, as the bearings for these were not as close or efficient a fit as they had been prior to the collision with the *Hawke*.

The big secret

Although the postponement of the *Titanic*'s completion date allowed the necessary alterations to the ship that was to masquerade as her, how could Harland and Wolff keep this great fraud a secret? Although Britain was still two years away from a war with Germany, the shipyard was able to invoke the Official Secrets Act, which meant that anything that took place within the Belfast shipyard stayed inside it. How on earth could Harland and Wolff get away with citing the Official Secrets Act? Well, this would have required the connivance of the British Government in the 'switch'. Surely this was not possible? But suppose, with the possibility of a major war becoming increasingly likely, Britain urgently needed large troop carriers capable of defending themselves while they delivered arms and men to any theatre of war? For obvious political reasons, the British Government could not be seen to be spending untold millions of public money building ships designed for a war that no one was officially recognising as a possibility. Also, news that Britain was equipping itself with huge armed troop carriers would have immediately encouraged Germany to do likewise.

A picture tells a story

My grandfather, the Reverend Hannah, was well aware of the talk amongst those who worked in the Northern Ireland shipbuilding industry, some of whom were either his parishioners or at least related to them. Sometimes, when we were alone, the talk between Grandfather Hannah and me as a small boy turned to ships and the sea. Although not a sailor himself, Canon Hannah had lived close by the sea for most of his life and knew and understood both those who built ships and those who sailed in them; although, when he talked about 'the great ship', it was beyond my ability as a six-year-old to grasp what my Irish grandfather meant when he said, 'Ask my friend, the harbour master, Mr Waters about that ship – ah, but then he's long gone.'

And then he would clam up about it. My mother certainly seemed to have no idea what he was talking about and yet, according to Grandfather Hannah, as a teenager, she had been with him and the Ardglass harbour master, John Waters, watching the tugs pulling *Titanic* slowly and sedately down the Lagan river as Waters remarked to my grandfather, as he snapped pictures of the ship, that there was 'something strange' about her.

Unfortunately, Waters, like Grandfather Hannah, is long gone and with him I fear, his photographic collection. Perhaps there is a relative somewhere who still has these interesting shots and, if so, I would certainly love to see them.

Reasons to be doubtful

By February 28th 1912, the *Olympic* was back in Harland and Wolff's Belfast yard, as a number of the rivets around the damaged part of the hull were failing. So on March 6th 1912, the *Olympic* that sailed out of the yards was actually the *Titanic*. As the *Olympic*, she would sail the seas for a further twenty-three years, almost certainly a technical impossibility for the now fatally flawed real *Olympic*.

The owners of the newly launched *Titanic* claimed that the carpeting in the First Class restaurant of their supership was a luxurious improvement on the linoleum tiles of the *Olympic*. However, when James Cameron, in his submersible vehicle, sent his ultra-small, ultra-manoeuvrable remote video camera deep into the heart of the sunken ship, there in what had been the First Class restaurant were revealed – lino tiles beneath the rotted carpet! Lino tiles under a carpet? Of course, the lino tiles of the old *Olympic* would never have looked new, as the ship had already been carrying passengers to and fro across the Atlantic. So the easiest, and more importantly the quickest way to handle this was to lay carpet over the top of the worn tiles. There was no time for anything else when there was such a rush to make the 'switch' from *Olympic* to *Titanic*.

Who wants to go on a maiden voyage?

Surprisingly, there were comparatively few people travelling on the *Titanic*'s maiden voyage, considering it was trumpeted as being the most desirable luxury vessel ever created. The *Titanic*, as she was now known, was designed to carry a full complement of over two thousand people, but only 1,316 appear to have actually booked a passage. So, almost a thousand potential passengers elected not to go on the ship's first voyage. Certainly, there are those who prefer not to make a journey on a ship's first trip, preferring to wait until any little faults that may arise have been ironed out. However, one thousand unsold tickets – surely rather strange, considering the supposed importance of this liner? Perhaps word had in fact leaked out in certain circles that there was – as the Ardglass harbour master, John Waters, remarked – something 'strange' about this ship?

Ghost ships

At this point, it's worth noting that the *Carpathia* – which was to play such a key role in the rescue of the *Titanic*'s survivors – was, although a smaller vessel, capable of carrying almost as many passengers. This ship, under the command of Captain Arthur Rostron, bound from New York to Europe, was due to pass the *Titanic* on its maiden voyage somewhere off the shallow Grand Banks of Newfoundland.

As the *Carpathia* was getting ready to leave New York, another ship, the *Californian*, was preparing to play her part in the drama, prior to sailing from London. Both ships were unexpectedly loaded with blankets and warm clothing, yet carried very few passengers. In the haste to get the *Californian* out to sea the wireless operator brought the wrong charts on board. Thus he was unable to tell at any point during the voyage across the Atlantic exactly what ships were near and at what range. This is just one of the many unfortunate mistakes that in all probability contributed to the *Titanic* fraud going disastrously wrong with such a huge loss of life.

In the two weeks prior to her first and, as it turned out, only voyage, *Titanic*, as we shall call her, was a hive of activity. Strangely enough J. P. Morgan, who was booked to sail on the ship's maiden voyage, travelling in one of her most luxurious staterooms, decided at the last moment not to go. Although Morgan cited illness for this cancellation, a diligent newspaper reporter managed to track him down to the South of France at this time, where he was secreted with his current mistress – and not looking at all unwell! None of Morgan's precious artefacts travelled on the *Titanic* either, as Second Officer Lightoller duly noted in his task of ensuring all cargo was properly and securely stowed in the giant liner's holds.

So, if there was a *Titanic* scam afoot, who knew about it? Certainly the following would have to have known: starting at the top of the tree of culpability, J. P. Morgan and J. Bruce Ismay, closely followed by the senior people at Harland and Wolff and then, of course, the three senior officers aboard the ship who had all served on the *Olympic* and knew her well – namely Captain Smith, Chief Officer Wilde and First Officer Murdoch. There is no way that these experienced seamen would not know what ship they were on.

Insuring *Titanic*

The *Titanic/Olympic* was insured for four million pounds, so if she disappeared beneath the waves and no blame for this was attached to either the company or the ship's officers, then the White Star Line, and hence J. P. Morgan, stood to make a very considerable profit out of the loss. It would certainly get Ismay and White Star out of the financial hole that the crippling of the real *Olympic* had caused.

It was only after *Titanic*'s sea trials in Belfast Lough that Henry Wilde was drafted in as First Officer, causing the last-minute reshuffle of the other officers and loss of the vital binoculars. First Officer Wilde never set foot on board the *Titanic* until the morning of April 10th 1912. Yet before the ship started across the Atlantic for the first and last time, Wilde sent a letter ashore to be posted to his sister. In it he apparently quite clearly stated: 'I still do not like the ship.' How could this possibly be? Unless he was only too aware that the ship in question was in fact the *Olympic* on which he had previously served as Chief Officer.

Choosing the wrong route

Standing orders of the White Star Line forbade their ships from taking the 'autumn southern route' after mid March, because of the danger of icebergs. Captain Smith chose to take this route rather than the 'outward south' one which would be less likely to encounter ice. Surely neither he nor any of those intending to sink the false *Titanic* planned to actually hit an iceberg?

Whatever the reason, it was yet another blunder in the fatal catalogue of carelessness that caused the unnecessary loss of life.

An extremely mild winter in Greenland in 1911 had meant that there were more gigantic pieces of ice, some almost as big as a small mountain, breaking off from the polar ice cap and drifting south.

Warnings that went unheeded

From early on the morning of April 14th 1912, messages carrying ice warnings were picked up by the *Titanic*.

We know that Ismay carried a vital telegram, warning of ice ahead, around in his pocket for some time before it finally reached the duty officers. We know he showed it to Marian Thayer, the lady he had apparently fallen suddenly and desperately in love with, despite the fact that she was travelling to New York in the company of her husband and her son, Jack. Was Ismay mad? Did he actually want to hit an iceberg or was this just another disastrous blunder? Could it all be part of some monumental fraud that went horribly and tragically wrong?

It would be easy to dismiss the suggestion of a deliberate sinking with the loss of over fifteen hundred people as extremely unlikely – except that the revealing of recent major frauds makes clear that, when it comes to big business, sheer greed will drive men to any lengths, and take any risk, in the hope of making obscene profits. Bernie Madoff's sixty-five-billion-dollar Ponzi scheme; Enron's false accounting of eleven billion dollars' worth of shareholders' money, resulting in the dissolution of Arthur Andersen, one of the world's largest accountancy firms; the list is almost endless. The only difference is that all or most modern-day corporate fraudsters get found out sooner or later, but a hundred years ago the deliberate sinking of a luxury liner was simply inconceivable as a possible fraud.

Chapter 22
Who sank the ship?

Fraud at sea

The English Marine Insurance Act of 1907 states:

> Subject to the provisions of this Act, and in the absence of fraud, the value fixed by the policy is, as between the insurer and the assured, conclusive of the insurable value of the subject intended to be insured.

This is particularly relevant, as we know that the White Star Line had a high premium to pay for insuring the *Titanic*, but then – it was only for half a voyage! There are plenty of examples of actions that support the likelihood of an intentional sinking, including the classic example of the sinking of the infamous tanker *Salem* off Africa in 1977. Here the entire crew were found in good spirits with all their belongings in lifeboats while the ship was still sinking. There was no trace on the water, as the ship sank, of the full cargo of oil, stated to have been on board but which had already been sold. The scuttling of the vessel became too obvious for the fraudsters to even press an insurance claim. But the circumstances are seldom so obvious.

The *Tropaiforos* sank in the Bay of Bengal. The insurer alleged that water had been pumped in through bilge lines and ballast lines, while the owner insisted that the vessel had hit an unidentified object. The crew's testimonies were highly inconsistent, with different statements as to the side on which the vessel had been leaking, and it appeared that the radio operator had sent a Mayday message before the alleged moment of hitting the alleged object!

The details of some maritime frauds are actually more amusing than tragic. For instance, when the *Spathari36* grounded and sank off the Portuguese coast in such calm weather that even small boats could come out and give assistance, the ship's captain, when asked why he had not sent for help, replied: 'It slipped my memory.'

Of course the sinking of the ship known as the *Titanic* was certainly no laughing matter; although, had the fraud gone according to plan and all aboard been safely rescued, there would no doubt have been some self-congratulatory smiles in the White Star Boardroom.

Titanic's last hours

On the night of April 14th–15th, several strange things happened. Chief Officer Wilde, on Captain Smith's orders, altered the ship's course. The direction they were now heading in would take them straight into the area where they had already been warned that ice had been found. At six in the evening Wilde handed over the bridge to Second Officer Lightoller. Great Uncle Bertie must have known that he was now sailing a ship on a course that was heading straight into an area of icebergs.

Earlier in the evening Lightoller had overheard Ismay and Thomas Andrews, the Managing Director of Harland and Wolff, in a heated discussion over dinner about the state of the starboard engine which was vibrating violently, caused of course by the ill-fitting bearings on the *Olympic*, as she really was. Of course it is perfectly possible that, even at this point, my great uncle had not yet put a simple two and two together and arrived at four, and so guessed that he was not aboard the brand new *Titanic* but the rather battered *Olympic*; although how a seaman with twenty years' experience of sailing the world's oceans, thirteen of them with White Star Lines, could fail to 'smell a rat' beggars belief.

A question of lookouts

Apparently it would have been easier to spot an iceberg from a position lower down than in the crow's nest: ideally in the bows of the ship, as pointed out by Sir Ernest Shackleton at the London Board of Trade Inquiry. Yet no lookouts were placed anywhere other than in the crow's nest, even allowing for the fact that the *Titanic* was fast approaching an area known to contain icebergs. However, while on his watch on the ship's final night, Lightoller sent repeated instructions to the two men in the crow's nest to 'keep a sharp lookout for ice'. This surely shows that he must have been concerned about the whole situation of visibility. The lack of a lookout in the bows of the ship, plus Lightoller's inability to provide binoculars, may well have contributed to the fatal collision.

The last ship to see the doomed *Titanic* was the *Rappahannoch* which, as it passed within signalling distance, sent a message by Morse lamp: 'Have just passed through heavy field of ice and icebergs.' Although the *Titanic* acknowledged this message, there was no suggestion of her slowing down as she entered the danger zone.

Why did the *Californian* stop?

Meanwhile the *Californian*, which had made all possible speed in its transatlantic journey so far, now apparently stopped some fifty miles from the White Star Liner. According to her commander, Captain Lord, this was to avoid sailing into an ice field in the dark – possibly a somewhat overcautious decision for a ship in such an apparent hurry.

Although Great Uncle Bertie claimed to have been in his cabin at the time of the collision, he stated to one of the inquiries afterwards that there was no haze or mist that night, an apparent attempt to discredit the lookouts. One wonders how he could have known the prevailing weather conditions at the time of the collision when he was supposedly below decks at the time in question.

When the crow's nest lookouts finally sighted a giant iceberg full ahead, the ship was still some ten miles away from it. However, for whatever reason, the Officer of the Watch, First Officer Murdoch, was not present on the bridge when Reginald Lee rang through from the crow's nest with the vital news. By the time Murdoch had finally heard the bridge phone ringing, *Titanic* was steaming, almost at her maximum speed, towards the iceberg which was now perilously close. Murdoch panicked and ordered 'Hard a-starboard!' and called for the engines to be reversed to 'Full a-stern!'

If the story that my second cousin, Louise Patten, tells in her book *Good as Gold* is correct, the helmsman turned the wrong way and, seeing the error, Murdoch grabbed the wheel – but all too late. The great vessel scraped the iceberg as she veered away.

How to sink a ship

As Robin Gardiner explains in his book *The Great Titanic Conspiracy*, there has long been a standard procedure for scuttling a ship: that is to say, the deliberate and planned sinking of a vessel.

> Simply opening the sea cocks does not guarantee that a vessel will flounder; the accepted method is usually to open the sea cocks but also reverse the non-return valves on the ship's pumps, so that instead of pumping water out, they pump it in... Using this method the sinking is at least under some sort of control... If some of the *Titanic*'s pumps had been set to scuttle the ship, that might account for Captain Smith's reluctance to have them started when a real catastrophe overtook his vessel.

As the first thing that Murdoch did on seeing the approaching iceberg was to order 'Full a-stern' in a ship of over forty-six thousand tons travelling at over 20 knots, the sudden reverse of engines would have undoubtedly thrown a huge shudder through the entire ship. It then appears that, once Captain Smith had appeared on the bridge, the *Titanic* was put full ahead and then full astern at least one or more times.

Iceberg or mystery ship?

The received story of the *Titanic*'s demise, accepted for the past hundred years, is that the ship hit an iceberg and sank in one of the deepest parts of the Atlantic Ocean. However, Robin Gardiner's *The Great Titanic Conspiracy* suggests some interesting theories that are worth exploring. Witnesses of the event suggested that the iceberg in question was over one hundred feet tall, one person even likening it to the Rock of Gibraltar. Estimates thus put the huge iceberg's weight at around half a million tons or more; that is to say, almost ten times the weight of *Titanic*. Robin Gardiner says:

> Even at better than 20 knots, *Titanic* was not going to push this iceberg out of the way. She would just bounce off it, like a tennis ball off a wall. The change in direction of the ship's travel would necessarily have been violent and practically instant. Any almost instantaneous change in the ship's course would have been noticed by all aboard. Most of those in the forward part of the ship, closest to the point of impact, and therefore closer to the point of deflection, would have felt a severe shock to the extent that they would have been thrown off their feet. Articles on tables would have fallen off as they tried to continue along the vessel's previous heading. According to Newton's first law of motion, if the iceberg was moving in a southerly direction at approximately 2 knots (roughly the speed of the Labrador Current that was driving it) and the *Titanic* was heading in a westerly direction at about 22 knots the collision would be but a glancing blow, hardly felt in a ship of that size.

The various testimonies and accounts from the survivors of the sinking almost unanimously attest to a slight jar or scrape, nothing more; certainly not a monstrous object tearing a gaping hole from stem to stern in a ship where, as Gardiner points out:

> All the joints in the hull plating were double, triple or even quadruple riveted, with about a million rivets – the largest being one and a quarter inches in diameter – going into the construction of each vessel (*Titanic* and *Olympic* were built simultaneously). The six-inch-wide hull plates overlapped one another by at least six inches along all the horizontal joints. The ship was extremely strong.

A glancing blow

Assuming this was the patched-up *Olympic*, it should be remembered that she had not sunk when rammed and severely holed by HMS *Hawke*, a Royal Navy cruiser. So, probably this previously damaged vessel was still strong enough to stay afloat after a glancing blow from an iceberg. Gardiner explains just where, if at all, the ship was wounded:

> Lamp Trimmer Samuel Hemmings noticed a peculiar hissing sound very shortly after the accident. He investigated and discovered the noise was air escaping from the forepeak water tank as it filled from below. The forepeak water tank was situated low down in the bows of the ship, and had seemingly been opened to the sea by the collision.

Gardiner later quotes the United States Hydrographic Office's calculations relative to the amount of force required to have inflicted the alleged rip in the *Titanic*'s side:

> To have opened a half-inch slit over a length of some three hundred and fifty-five feet in the vessel's side, 1,178,200 foot tons of energy would have been required, enough to physically throw the whole ship twenty feet sideways. This amount of energy is comparable to the liner being struck by a full broadside from a contemporary battleship, yet hardly anybody noticed anything!

Had the hole in the ship's hull been caused by a piece of ice protruding from an iceberg, the impact would have broken off pieces of the berg. However, there were no reports of any ice whatsoever inside the ship; only what was said to have cascaded onto the forward well deck. But this was shortly after the engines had been thrust into reverse while the liner was travelling forward at 20 knots or more. In the freezing north Atlantic night, ice would easily have formed on the ship's rigging and been shaken off the foremast as the engines suddenly reversed causing the entire vessel to shudder.

Marian Thayer and the mystery ship

Marian Thayer, the object of Ismay's unrequited love, is quoted as saying later that, after a possible collision:

> Whilst still on the boat deck I saw what appeared to be the hull of a ship heading in the opposite direction to our ship and quite near us, from which rockets were being sent up. The vessel, about a mile off by this time, was half the size of the *Cedric* and higher out of the water than the *Carpathia*.

The *Cedric* was another White Star vessel that Marian Thayer was obviously familiar with, while the *Carpathia* was of course the rescue ship that transported Mrs Thayer and her son Jack to New York, her husband having gone down with the *Titanic*. She also adds that:

> Upon looking over the side of the vessel, I saw what looked like a number of long black ribs, apparently floating nearly level with the surface of the water. These long, black objects were parallel with the side of the ship.

As it was a dark, moonless night, the objects that Marian Thayer saw must have been very close to the *Titanic* and thus illuminated by the lights from the liner's portholes. So, what was the mystery ship and, if damaged by the *Titanic*, how badly was she damaged? Robin Gardiner poses the question:

Is it possible that a relatively small hull break reaching more than 15 feet into the interior of the liner could have been caused by her brushing alongside the rear end of another ship?

To which he answers simply: 'Yes' – explaining that the short, exposed propeller shaft of a much smaller vessel could have sliced into the *Titanic*'s hull like a stiletto. He further points out that this scenario would in no way contradict suggestions by survivors that something, assumed to be an iceberg, sliced into the *Titanic*.

Why not start the pumps?

The question was later asked as to why Captain Smith did not order the ship's pumps to be started the moment that he realised a collision had occurred and had been informed that water was entering the ship. In fact, he waited a further forty-five minutes before giving the order. If, as now seems a very real possibility, the ship was destined to be sunk in a controlled scuttle, the pumps, which had been reversed, could have done the job in a slow, controlled manner – but not, however, if the ship had already been holed before starting to deliberately flood her. To make matters worse, even forty-five minutes after the collision, Smith was still unaware that some of his junior engineers had taken matters into their own hands immediately after the collision and started some of the pumps in the forward part of the ship.

First Officer Murdoch had for some reason given the helmsman the order to turn the ship south as soon as he heard that there was an iceberg directly ahead. Had he ordered 'Hard a-port!' the *Titanic* would have turned towards the north, in the direction of where the *Californian* lay with engines stopped. However, by the time the *Titanic* finally halted her progress, she was some twenty miles from the nearest possible ship for immediate rescue.

Perhaps Great Uncle Bertie may not at this point have been fully aware of the situation. However, he probably knew that the ship was sinking and that the lifeboats, which he had tested in such a perfunctory manner on Belfast Lough, would only carry about half the number of people currently aboard the doomed liner.

An awful lot of people were not going to make it.

Chapter 23
A recipe for disaster

The mystery deepens

A coal strike in Britain had resulted in many liners being
unable to put to sea, as their steam-driven engines consumed a
great deal of coal, especially on a transatlantic trip; yet the
Californian was a Leyland Line ship and that company was
owned by – yes, you guessed it – J. P. Morgan's IMM. Unlike
most other liners in the Port of London, the *Californian* did
not seem short of coal; and yet despite the fact that, as a result
of this, she had for the moment cornered the market, not a
single passenger sailed in her when she set off for her date with
destiny.

As the *Californian* lay almost motionless on the edge of an
ice field on the night of April 14th–15th 1912, several sightings
were made by her officers of a mystery ship, too small to be a
liner and thought to be a tramp steamer. Repeated efforts with
a Morse Lamp to contact this other ship received no reply.

There was also the complex question of the rockets. *Titanic*
definitely fired a series of distress rockets, which were rather
more like mortar shells, bursting with a bright, white light and
a loud explosion. Officers aboard the *Californian* saw what
they thought were either shooting stars or possibly rockets
from a ship. There seems to have been general disagreement as
to what exactly these lights were. Certainly no immediate
action was taken as a result of these sightings.

The call goes unanswered

Cyril Evans, the overworked radio operator on the *Californian*, went to bed at about 11.30 on this particular night but was awoken by Third Officer Grove, for whom the relatively new process of radio contact at sea was something he was particularly fascinated by. He had some understanding of the Morse code and of the Marconi Company's equipment. But of course he was not a qualified operator like Evans, who told Grove that the only ship around was the *Titanic*, which he judged to be about a hundred miles away. When Grove switched on the wireless apparatus and placed the headphones on, he heard nothing. Evans, who had by then gone back to sleep, had failed to remind the Third Officer to wind up the signal detector, a primitive but nevertheless effective way of tracking other ships. As it was, *Titanic*'s distress calls went unanswered.

For some apparently unaccountable reason, the Commander of the *Californian*, Captain Lord, who was well over six feet tall, chose to spend that particular night fully dressed on a rather short settee in the chart room, rather than on the more comfortable bunk in his cabin. It must have been an extremely uncomfortable night and it suggests that he was prepared for some kind of emergency.

No lifeboat drill

Meanwhile, back on board the *Titanic*, Captain Smith ordered the officers to prepare the lifeboats. Just after midnight on April 15th, the first wireless distress signals were sent out from the *Titanic*, but the ship's position had been wrongly calculated when Lightoller read the stars to Boxhall. Once the calculations had been remade and a true position arrived at, this was broadcast and picked up by the *Carpathia*, sixty miles away. On receipt of these distress calls, her Commander, Captain Rostron, was immediately roused from his bed. He ordered the ship to turn around and make all speed in the direction of the confirmed sinking. As the ship, whose cruising speed was 14 knots, raced through the ocean at something approaching 18 knots, everything aboard shook with the vibration of the overworked engines.

Carpathia to the rescue

The *Carpathia* quickly became the scene of speedy but organised preparations for the anticipated rescue operation. Blankets were collected, passengers gave up their cabins to accommodate survivors, and Captain Rostron posted extra lookouts on the bridge, in the crow's nest and in the extreme bows of the ship. All obstructions were cleared from the decks and gangways, while nets and rope ladders were prepared to help the fittest of those to be rescued climb aboard the *Carpathia*.

Captain Rostron drove his ship through a dark, moonless night, directly into an ice field at well above his proper speed, constantly adjusting his course to avoid a series of bergs. He knew from his wireless operator that there were no other ships anywhere near, apart from the doomed *Titanic*; so that, should his own ship hit an iceberg, there would be no one to rescue her either.

Truth and the *Carpathia*

This is the story told by Rostron and his officers, on the basis of which the Captain became a public hero and was awarded the US Congressional Gold medal. In fact, his career had been very much in the doldrums prior to the *Titanic* disaster, and the *Carpathia* was by no means Cunard's premier liner. Yet his apparent heroism in 1912 meant that he was later knighted by a grateful King and Country and, before his retirement in 1931, Rostron became Commodore of the Cunard Fleet. So, as they say, 'It's an ill wind that blows nobody any good.'

Sir Ernest Shackleton made it quite clear during his appearance before the British Board of Trade Inquiry that to travel at anything other than a greatly reduced speed in a known Atlantic ice field was truly foolhardy. Would Rostron have risked the lives of his crew and passengers, as well as his own life and that of his ship, in a desperate effort to reach a sinking liner some sixty miles distant? Or was the *Carpathia* actually less than half that distance from the *Titanic*, when she was in distress? To add to the mystery, it turns out that before leaving New York the *Carpathia* had spent time in a Brooklyn shipyard having her public rooms prepared for easy use as dormitories or even hospital wards. The ship had also taken on board extra blankets and not one but seven doctors. The outbreak of World War I was still over two years away, yet this Cunard ship appeared to be equipped to enter a war zone.

There are many mysteries surrounding the sinking of the *Titanic* and not the least of these are the 'mystery ships' seen from the bridge of the stricken liner. When the Morse signals flashed at the two ships failed to receive a reply, Great Uncle Bertie is reported to have remarked that he wished he had a six-inch gun, so he could put a shot into one of the mystery ships and wake her up!

Captain Smith's final mistake

Captain Smith was so convinced that there was another ship close by – certainly within just a few miles – that he instructed the crew to lower two of the lifeboats and row some passengers to this other ship and then, having transferred them, return to pick up more. Robin Gardiner in *The Great Titanic Conspiracy* believes that Captain Smith was expecting rescue ships to be on hand when he scuttled the *Titanic*:

> If Smith and his officers believed that this particular mystery ship was there to rescue them it would make sense of their allowing the few lifeboats available to leave *Titanic* only partly full of people.

This theory begs the question – was my great uncle so angry at the mystery ship he sighted because he was expecting a rescue that for some extraordinary reason did not go according to plan?

Who was in command of this mystery ship? And why did he not attempt to rescue the passengers and crew of the *Titanic*? Robin Gardiner's book contains a chilling suggestion:

> There has to be some compelling reason why this mysterious vessel did nothing. All sailors have a built-in disposition to help others on the sea. Even in wartime, seamen go to extraordinary lengths to rescue people from enemy vessels which they have shortly before been doing battle with. In the case of the *Titanic*, there was no apparent physical danger to a would-be rescuer if it was already close by. So perhaps the danger was not physical. If the Captain of the mystery ship was already party to the plan to scuttle the *Titanic*, but could see for himself that the plan had gone awry, he might well have considered it prudent to keep away.

I must say that I find the suggestion of such heartlessness rather hard to swallow; and yet human beings behave in such strange and unpredictable ways when in extreme situations that perhaps there is some truth in this theory after all. Certainly, from the extraordinary and long-remembered episode of the *Titanic*'s sinking emerged a whole host of unanswered questions, the answers to some of which Great Uncle Bertie took with him to his grave.

A hero with 'feet of clay'?

Great Uncle Bertie certainly made some wild assertions when cross-examined at the US Senate Inquiry, especially when it came to the subject of lifeboats. Of his own admission, these had not been fully and satisfactorily tested during the ship's sea trials. It was his contention that the wooden lifeboats would buckle in the middle, if lowered from the boat deck to the sea with a full complement of passengers in them. This was manifestly untrue, as many of the last boats lowered from the *Titanic* were filled to capacity and survived the descent to the water below without breaking. In the chaos of lowering the boats, my great uncle encountered a number of problems which delayed his part in the evacuation process. Whether this was due to his incompetence and lack of proper knowledge or whether there were actual design faults involved is not clear.

An example of the shambles that Second Officer Lightoller was caught up in is evident from records describing a serious discrepancy in the lowering of boats number 11 and 12 at approximately 1.25am on the fateful morning. First Officer Murdoch managed to squeeze some seventy people into boat number 11, whilst Second Officer Lightoller was happy to see boat number 12 lowered away with only forty-three in it.

We know that there was a set of emergency boats kept permanently swung out and ready for any occasion. Lightoller found that one of these boats, number 2, had not been lowered earlier in the proceedings and was full of what he described as 'dagoes'. He quickly threatened to shoot them with his revolver unless they gave up their place to those he considered to be of a more deserving nature, apparently referring to First Class passengers. This rough-and-ready approach, which today we might consider fascistic, was perhaps not at all surprising from a rough-and-ready sea dog like Lightoller. Still, it doesn't show my great uncle in a very good light. And yet, like Captain Rostron of the *Carpathia*, he became a public hero and was later awarded the Distinguished Service Cross during World War I.

What did Grandma Gertrude not tell me?

Great Uncle Bertie was loved and admired by many. Driven to discover whether the great family hero did in fact have 'feet of clay', I have spent long days, weeks and months seeking to unearth the true picture of that terrible night when the hopes and dreams of a nation sank beneath a cruel, dark sea. For a century now, writers and researchers, students and oceanographers, survivors and their descendents, the press, the media and the maritime world in general have all, like me, searched to find the definitive answer to apparently unanswerable questions.

As a young boy, Grandma Gertrude made some strange remarks. What exactly did she mean by: 'The sea is a place of mysteries – and there are mystery ships upon it'?

Many years later, in my detailed researches about a possible maritime fraud of unimaginable complexity and ruthlessness, I came across more than one witness referring to 'mystery ships'. Yet the identity of these ships is as unknown today as it was on that terrible night one hundred years ago. Grandma Gertrude, when teaching me the rudiments of painting, told me that: 'Life is a series of impressions.'

Was that an attempt to encourage me to copy some of the techniques of the great French Impressionists – or was it also to suggest, once again, that in life all is not always what it seems? When she took me out into her garden all those years ago, she told me that I said the sky was blue because I had always been told that it was blue and hence believed it. And yet, she showed me that it was not blue at all. So perhaps millions of people have, for the past one hundred years, said that the *Titanic* hit an iceberg because that is exactly what they have been told happened.

Outside the box

In trying to find out more about Great Uncle Bertie and his involvement in the sinking of the *Titanic*, I have been forced to think 'outside the box'. Nevertheless, my researches for this book have uncovered some extraordinary reports. These include:

- Lawrence Beesley's account of the excessive vibrations in the ship (caused, I believe, by an engine out of alignment) in his book *The Loss of the SS Titanic*.
- James Cameron's discovery of the marble surround in Ismay's stateroom in the wrecked *Titanic* matching exactly that in the *Olympic*.
- Robert Ballard's photos of the wreck, clearly showing the propeller shaft originally 'borrowed' from *Titanic* and used

on the *Olympic*; the relevant number, 401, is clear for all to see.

- The 'patch' of paint on the *Titanic* that didn't match that on the rest of the ship, indicating the presence of the repair to the *Olympic* after her collision with HMS *Hawke*.
- Videos of the floor of the wreck's restaurant, showing rotten carpet revealing worn lino tiles beneath it – not what you would expect to find on a brand-new ship.
- The three most senior officers on the *Titanic*'s maiden voyage all having come straight off the *Olympic* – Captain Smith, Chief Officer Wilde and First Officer Murdoch.
- Murdoch's letter to his wife, immediately before the start of the *Titanic*'s maiden voyage, saying: 'I never liked this ship' – yet he had only just been seconded to the *Titanic*, so he must have thought that the *Titanic* was really his old ship, the *Olympic*.

So, why did Grandma Gertrude keep the *Titanic* newspaper clippings? Sentiment? Morbid interest? Or something more? I never did find out. My meetings with Great Uncle Bertie were always in the company of my parents and his wife, Great Aunt Sylvia. He certainly seemed to me, as a young impressionable boy, to be a tough old nut.

And was there some hidden message in the dialogue I had with Grandma Gertrude immediately after the Commander's funeral?

'What a terrible loss,' she said. But then when I asked, 'You mean Great Uncle Bertie?' she replied, 'Yes, but all those other innocent souls who died – and all unnecessarily.'

Of course it could just be that, based on the mysteries I have unearthed in my recent researches, I am reading more than intended into her remarks to me as a twelve-year-old boy. But I don't think so. When she presented me with the Lightoller coat of arms it almost felt like some kind of ceremonial occasion, as if I was being admitted to the Ancient Order of Lightollers! I suppose that, when you are part of an ancient and venerable family, whatever scandals and crimes are committed by its members, the family's 'good name' is something the descendants of the line will automatically strive to protect, no matter what. So perhaps that's why Grandma Gertrude only ever dropped subtle hints of what her brother's real relationship was with the ill-fated *Titanic*.

Although my mother Elizabeth was a Lightoller and the Commander was her uncle, I feel that there may have been cover-ups of unimaginable proportions where the life and death of the *Titanic* is concerned. So am I failing to uphold the family's 'good name'? Perhaps; but, as Christopher Columbus discovered, once embarked upon a voyage of discovery it is very hard to turn back.

We are all human

And then there was another telling remark of Grandma Gertrude's: 'Most people thought my brother was a hero. Well, in a way he was; but after all – we're all human.'

And 'human' is what most of the people involved displayed themselves to be, on board *Titanic* in the early hours of the morning of April 15th 1912. Great Uncle Bertie was undoubtedly heroic in some of his acts. Yet he was also possibly inefficient and ineffective in others.

Afterword

What the public wants

The story told in film and on television was always the one that the public, and the powers that be, wanted us to hear: a disaster movie involving glamorous, rich people in a horrific nightmare situation – although there are also many excellent documentary films around that tell convincingly of the possible maritime fraud to end all frauds. But these remain on the fringe of the public's perception, because once the public has been 'sold' a great story, they just don't want to buy a different one.

Big ideas

In the last hundred years or so our material world has developed at 'warp speed', compared to the progress made in previous centuries. This includes our conquest of the oceans. J. Bruce Ismay's vision of the White Star Line being crowned supreme ruler of the transatlantic run drove him to overreach himself and his company.

Everyone, from the highest to the lowest, was swept along by the sheer grandeur of the concept – three giant ships: palaces on the high seas. Who could resist such an awe-inspiring idea? The world needs big men with big ideas and J. Bruce Ismay, at six feet four, was a big man in every sense of the word. His ideas were big too, backed by the deep pockets of an ego even bigger than his own – J. Pierpont Morgan. A man whose wealth and power still couldn't make him immortal: for the year after the *Titanic* sank, he too left this world for ever.

Thrust into centre stage

Prior to the actual sinking of the *Titanic*, Great Uncle Bertie was just a small-part player in the drama of great ships. However, from the moment the giant vessel began to flounder, his role grew until, by the time he appeared in front of the official US and British inquiries, he had well and truly taken centre stage. He found himself, not of his own making, exposed in the spotlight of fame.

As the most senior surviving officer of the sinking, he should have presented a noble and heroic figure, restrained in his mourning for the men and the ship he had come to love. However, what both the transcripts of the inquiries and his autobiography *Titanic and Other Ships* present to us is a downright rude and difficult man with little or no tolerance for authority. Certainly we must allow for the terrible ordeal he had just been through; but surely a lifetime of service at sea would have engendered in him some innate sense of respect for the worthy men attempting to get to the bottom of a mysterious accident that had so shocked the world?

Or was there something more sinister about his behaviour? What do we know of the hours and days on board the rescue ship, *Carpathia*? We do know that Second Officer Lightoller spent time with J. Bruce Ismay, who had closeted himself in his cabin on that mournful voyage from the site of the drowned liner to New York. But what went on between these two men during that time? What kind of pressure did Ismay bring to bear on Lightoller? How much did Great Uncle Bertie know, or guess, of a possible attempted fraud of gigantic proportions? Did his boss let him in on the secret; and, if so, how did the Managing Director and Chairman of the White Star Line intend to buy this worthy officer's silence?

Even supposing that there was no intended fraud and that the horrific accident that befell the *Titanic* was purely due to the overconfidence of Ismay and the incompetence of the ship's officers and crew, Lightoller would still have been encouraged to phrase his answers to the official inquiries in the most ambiguous way possible. Was there a promised reward? Was it perhaps the command of a White Star Line ship? Could this ambitious officer have been persuaded to modify his version of the truth about the sinking?

However, at the end of the day there was no reward for the *Titanic*'s Second Officer. In fact, only the outbreak of World War I rescued him from sinking into almost total obscurity.

Saved by the war

The White Star Line returned Lightoller to the rank of First Officer on the *Oceanic*, not a patch on the majesty of the *Titanic* (or should that be *Olympic*?). However, Great Uncle Bertie was rescued from this somewhat ignominious position by the outbreak of the First World War.

No sooner had hostilities commenced than the Admiralty saw fit to exercise the option that they had long held with White Star to turn their ships into vehicles for the war effort. Within two weeks the *Oceanic* was swiftly converted into a man-o'-war, and Second Officer Lightoller of the White Star Line became Lieutenant Lightoller of His Majesty's Navy. For Great Uncle Bertie and the crew of the *Oceanic* the transformation was not a comfortable one. They felt they had not only been saddled with the unexplained and unwelcome jargon of the Royal Navy, but also its unnecessary forms of ranking and ceremony.

An unsuitable posting

Based among the far northern islands of Scotland, the great liner, now the property of the British Navy for the duration of the war, was totally unsuited to the narrow rocky channels of the area in which it was now based. The decision to operate a ship of her size in such dangerous waters was an accident just waiting to happen. And so it probably came as no surprise to my great uncle when the ship struck a reef and began to flounder. Great Uncle Bertie once again experienced a White Star Line vessel sinking beneath him. It was his third shipwreck – but this time without loss of life.

From the discomfort of a merchant ship unsuitably translated from a passenger carrier into a man-o'-war, Lieutenant Lightoller now found himself transferred by the Navy, in its unfathomable wisdom, to the role of Observer in one of the earliest military seaplanes, the Short 184. It was a role he did not enjoy, as the concept of landing and taking off on the deck of the cruiser *Campania* proved just that – a concept – rather than an absolute certainty!

From the sea, to the air and back to the sea again: at the end of 1915 Lightoller at last received a command of his own.

A ship of his own

Great Uncle Bertie was put in charge of a motor-torpedo boat, HMTB 117. This was at a time when German Zeppelins were causing severe casualties to British merchant shipping. Lightoller caught one of these hated airships in his gunner's sights and gave the order to fire. Although he claimed a hit, the Zeppelin is believed to have made it back to base but, as it were, with its tail between its legs. Nevertheless, for this perceived act of bravery, Great Uncle Bertie was decorated with the Distinguished Service Cross by the King and was given a new command: a torpedo-boat-destroyer, the *Falcon*.

Although this vessel saw very little action, Great Uncle Bertie managed to crash it into an Admiralty trawler, the *John Fitzgerald*. As he swam away from his sinking ship, suffering the fourth shipwreck of his seafaring career, he must have wondered how it was that he repeatedly had to 'jump' ship, whereas Conrad's *Lord Jim* and J. Bruce Ismay only had to do it once!

Vile sharks!

Great Uncle Bertie had a pathological hatred of German U-boats and he was determined to write off one or more of these submarines before he was done. The underwater marauders constantly attacked the defenceless merchant ships of the North Atlantic run and Lightoller hated them with a deep detestation, saying: 'They rank lower than the vilest sharks, and I've met a good few of them in my time.'

His loathing of these 'sharks' knew no bounds, as exemplified by another remark in his autobiography: a remark that today we should probably consider extremely racist and unfair, but then, as I have said before, he was a rough old sea dog!

> The man that could sink a merchantman, from below the surface, without giving him the ghost of a chance, must have had a mentality lower than the worst aborigine and heaven knows, they glory in some pretty filthy practices.

When depth charges from his latest command forced the German UB-110 to the surface, Lightoller rammed his vessel into her. The German submarine was finished but Great Uncle Bertie had critically damaged his own ship, this time a prized possession of His Majesty's Royal Navy. Somehow Lightoller managed to avoid yet another 'jump' from a ship and his vessel finally limped back to base.

For this rather cavalier duel with a German U-boat, Great Uncle Bertie received a bar to go with his Distinguished Service Cross and was promoted to Lieutenant Commander. However, he was also given command of a desk at the Admiralty, a position he hated so much that his constant complaining about it finally persuaded the Admiralty to relent and offer him another commission. However, the war ended before he could avail himself of this offer.

Returning to the White Star Line in peacetime, my great uncle hoped that they too would offer him his own command as, during his time in the Navy, he had grown accustomed to being captain of his own ship. However, all he was offered was First Officer aboard the *Celtic*.

No place for Lightoller

With Ismay having taken early retirement and J. P. Morgan dead, the White Star Line was under a completely new management and they were determined to be the new broom that swept very clean. So there was no place for Lightoller as a commander of any of their ships. After all, who would give a command to an officer so closely associated with the disastrous sinking of the *Titanic*?

Great Uncle Bertie was no longer a young man and the Great Depression was about to cast its giant shadow across all areas of business. He tried vainly to find work ashore, but with little or no success. A hero at sea is one thing, but an unemployed hero on land is quite another matter.

Finally, in desperation, Great Aunt Sylvia suggested that they open a boarding house; and, under her captaincy, it prospered with Great Uncle Bertie acting merely as a First Mate.

Sundowner

But the urge to be at sea again became an obsession. And from this came the birth of *Sundowner*, the family motor yacht, converted from an old Admiralty pinnace. Originally steam-driven, the Lightollers had her converted to a petrol-paraffin sixty-horsepower engine. From then on, every spring and summer holiday was spent aboard the newly converted yacht. They would regularly take her to France, Belgium and Holland, exploring the canals there with masts lowered to cruise beneath the many bridges.

Spies!

Then in 1939 came the longed-for chance of active service again, but this time of a very different nature. Lightoller was summoned to a highly secret meeting with a very senior naval officer. Naval Intelligence had a job for Great Uncle Bertie – a job as a spy!

His instructions were to cruise the German coast, in and out of the Friesian Islands, in *Sundowner*: noting conditions suitable for an amphibious invasion, as well as any possible signs of German naval preparation. He dutifully accepted the commission, as an adventure on the high seas was more befitting to his temperament than helping to run a bed-and-breakfast establishment. Sylvia insisted on accompanying him on this secret mission and it proved to be a wise move. As she steered their yacht around the German coast, Great Uncle Bertie was able to take photos of key locations through the portholes below decks. Taking soundings of the sea bed off the beaches had to be done at night under cover of darkness to avoid detection.

On one notable occasion a German naval patrol boat came uncomfortably close while Lightoller was photographing the coast from below. There was a holler though a loudhailer to Sylvia, busy knitting on deck, of: '*Wo ist der Kapitan?*' As the demand was repeated, Sylvia was relieved and amused when her husband staggered on deck waving a bottle of gin in one hand and a glass in the other. He exaggeratedly toasted the stern-looking commander of the patrol boat who, together with his crew, laughed at the drunken old yachtsman and sailed on their way. Great Uncle Bertie and his wife were never bothered again and completed their mission successfully; though whether or not the photos and data they had collected were ever put to good use by the Admiralty is unknown.

However, shortly after this World War II did in fact break out, bringing with it a terrible personal tragedy. The Lightollers' youngest son, Brian, who had joined the RAF, was killed on a bombing raid during the first night of the war.

Dunkirk

During the last days of May 1940, Britain suffered probably
her most ignominious defeat for many centuries. The nation
whose empire had spanned the known and unknown world
and painted the map red from one side of the globe to the
other was taking a terrible beating.

With France having fallen and the realisation that Calais to
Dover was but a short sea crossing for Hitler's war machine,
the quaintly named British Expeditionary Force sailed bravely
across the English Channel to teach the Hun a lesson.
Unfortunately the Hun was not in the mood for a lesson and
his fearsome defences ranged along France's coastline began to
scythe through the ranks of the invading British forces, as they
fell like newly cut corn.

When the call came it found Commander Lightoller
dressed as if for one of his regular cruises in the motor yacht
Sundowner; while beside him, as he adjusted the wheel to
manoeuvre the boat into the open sea, stood his ever-loyal
wife, Great Aunt Sylvia.

Lightoller was once again in charge of a ship bound for
adventure. The Commander set course for the French coast:
his objective, to ferry back to safety as many as possible of the
hundreds of British troops pinned down on the beaches of
Dunkirk by enemy guns and warplanes. Churchill's hastily
assembled armada of eight hundred and fifty 'little ships'
included not only the sixty-foot *Sundowner*, but commercial
vessels like pleasure craft, lifeboats and even Thames barges.
Great Uncle Bertie's charts of the English Channel were now
somewhat out of date; but new ones would have been of little
use, as the straits between England and France were now filled
with German mines and the wrecks of sunken vessels.

Back and forth went Great Uncle Bertie and Great Aunt
Sylvia, bringing some hundred and thirty British soldiers to
the safety of an English shore. Just one more adventure in an
adventurous life; although, in the eyes of the public, none of
his memorable exploits would ever eclipse the vital, yet

controversial role he played in the sinking of the most romantic and yet most unfortunate ship of all time – *Titanic*.

A legend again

It was June 1st 1940 and Great Uncle Bertie had become part of a legend again, acting as a lifesaver for those in mortal peril. But more tragedy was to come. With ghastly irony, his eldest son, Roger, was killed in the final month of the war while on active service with the Royal Navy.

Lux Vestra: Let Your Light Shine

Of course, as my twelve-year-old self watched the crematorium doors close on Great Uncle Bertie's coffin all those years ago, I knew almost nothing of the Commander's long and eventful life. It had been a life of adventure, shipwreck, bravery, mystery and unanswered questions. After a long and exhaustive investigation into the life and times of Commander Charles Herbert Lightoller, I must confess that I still cannot truly say whether he was a hero, an imperfect hero, or just someone reacting as best he could in the most extraordinary of circumstances.

I think we should let the old sea dog rest in peace; for, as Grandma Gertrude told me when I was a youngster: 'Most people thought that your Great Uncle Bertie was a hero. Well, in many ways he was; but after all – we're all human!'

Acknowledgements

I owe a debt of gratitude to my publisher, Dexter O'Neill, for prising out of me a story of adventure, heroism, villainy, family scandal and greed that has long hidden itself in the dark recesses of my mind.

Also, I can never thank my amazing wife Catherine enough for the invaluable support she has provided through untold hours of research, typing, cups of coffee and unfailing encouragement without which this book would never have got finished.

I am also indebted to all those who have gone before on this labyrinthine journey in attempting to get to the bottom of the mysteries surrounding the sinking of the *Titanic* and my great uncle's part in this. Although I may not be able to credit all the articles, blogs, YouTube videos, podcasts and studies that have helped me in my search for the truth about Great Uncle Bertie, I would particularly like to mention the invaluable aid I have received from reading the excellent books, *How to Survive the Titanic, or the Sinking of J. Bruce Ismay* by Frances Wilson and *The Great Titanic Conspiracy* by Robin Gardiner. Lawrence Beesley's 1912 first-hand account of the sinking, *The Loss of the SS Titanic: Its Story and its Lessons* was also a huge help.

References and further reading

The following books were used as sources of research in the writing of *Titanic ...And the Strange Case of Great Uncle Bertie*. I have marked with an asterisk the ones from which I have quoted directly.

*The Titanic Disaster Hearings: The Official Transcripts of the 1912 Senate Investigation
Tom Kuntz (editor), Pocket Books 1998

*Titanic and Other Ships
Commander C. H. Lightoller, Historia Press 2007 (first published by Ivor Nicholson and Watson 1935)

*How to Survive the Titanic, or the Sinking of J. Bruce Ismay
Frances Wilson, Bloomsbury 2011

*'Lights': The Odyssey of C. H. Lightoller
Patrick Stenson, Bodley Head 1984

*The Loss of the SS Titanic: Its Story and its Lessons
Lawrence Beesley, Forgotten Books 2008 (first published by Houghton Mifflin 1912)

*The Great Titanic Conspiracy
Robin Gardiner, Ian Allan 2010

Titanic: 9 Hours to Hell, The Survivors' Story
W. B. Bartlett, Amberley Publishing 2010

Lost Voices from the Titanic: The Definitive Oral History
Nick Barratt, Preface Publishing 2009

101 Things You Thought You Knew About the Titanic... But Didn't!
Tim Maltin, Beautiful Books 2010

Good as Gold: The Sinking of Titanic – What Really Happened
Louise Patten, Quercus 2010

Lord Jim
Joseph Conrad, Penguin Classics 2000 (first published by William Blackwood and Sons 1900)

Mary Baker Eddy: Christian Healer
Yvonne Caché von Fettweis and Robert Townsend Warneck, Christian Science Publishing Society 1998

*Science and Health with Key to the Scriptures
Mary Baker Eddy, Christian Science Board of Directors 2009